The Bookman

Art Seamans

To A GREAT
LADY

Fondly

The Bookman
Art A. Seamans

LIMEKILN BOOKS

SAN DIEGO, CALIFORNIA

First published by Limekiln Books, 2013

ISBN: 978-0-615-80077-6

Printed in the United States of America
San Diego, California

Acknowledgements

Many thanks are due my two assistants, April Anderson and Julie Randolph. Their expert language skills and computer knowledge, in addition to their enthusiastic spirits, have contributed much to this book. I wish also to thank proofreaders Kris De Young, Beverly Marvin and Tony Ross, proofreader and graphic designer Karen DeSollar and photographer Eddie Matthews.

Cover artwork by Issais Crow, assisted by student volunteers.

Dedication

This book is dedicated to the memory of Jack Grace and Leonard Pearlman. It is also dedicated to a number of others who have given much of themselves to the furtherance of The Bookman organization.

Table of Contents

Irwin Herman, the Bookman

CHAPTER 1

Getting on Board with the Bookman

"Dear Mr. Book mann. Tanky for all your stuped book. I don't like The reedinck book and do yo have a lot of book for read. I hate you because I dont like reading and this is real stuped to write to you because you don't exix yo are a fantancy Man. Sincerely, John Paul 1/22/02."

The Bookman laughed as he read this letter, which he claimed was his favorite. Indeed, the writer seemed to be right on in calling Irwin Herman a sort of fantasy man, a kind of Santa Claus, who had delivered presents (books) to the Job Corps program from which this man wrote the letter. Perhaps I should call the Bookman Father Winter since he is very proud of his Jewish heritage and would not see himself as a Christian saint. I could understand why this young man, the letter writer, was amazed that some man would, like Santa Claus, just deliver presents to anyone who wanted them or didn't want them, without asking anything in return. Although he could have played the role as a kind of Santa Claus, Mr. Irwin Herman, who read the letter to me, was no myth. In fact, he was a ball of energy, very much alive.

I found myself in a place that might have looked like Santa's North Pole workshop. How I got there is another story involving a touch of serendipity, a kind of magic. At her death, my neighbor Anita Johnson left behind a large number of books since she was a prolific reader. Her sister Janis had the task of disposing of Anita's books and magazines. Listening to the problem of where to get rid of these books, her automotive repairman on El Cajon Boulevard in the city of San Diego suggested that she donate the books to the Bookman and his enterprise, which stood a block away. Janis is an occasional visitor to our informal coffee klatch, and when she described briefly the Bookman and his venture, I became immediately intrigued and asked if I might go along on her next drop-off of books. When I arrived at the Bookman's warehouse on El Cajon Boulevard, what I saw and heard amazed me. I saw before me rows and rows of bookshelves packed with about 150,000 used books. Like an emperor in the middle of his vast domain, Irwin Herman described excitedly the accomplishments of this venture and his own philosophy, the two being intertwined.

The Bookman organization is the brainchild of Irwin Herman's imagination, concern, expertise and energy. He is quick to inform you that he is a seventy-nine-year-old Jew, a retired businessman from Chicago. Although he has been the subject of articles in local newspapers, most residents of San Diego, including me, had never heard of him. I thought of a line from Thomas Gray's "Elegy Written in a Country Churchyard"–"Full many a gem of purest ray serene/the dark unfathomed caves of ocean bear."

Although most residents of San Diego know nothing of the Bookman, there are many who do. That he is known by many is attested to by the fact that he has received many encomiums and awards. Irwin Herman is recognized by a number of prestigious educational organizations, such as the National Council of Teachers of English. Donors, both individuals and organizations, support this huge venture, and the walls of the warehouse are plastered with appreciative letters from hospitals, prisons, schools and foreign countries.

Herman interrupted my wondering gaze at the huge library before me by bombarding me with statistics detailing the extent of the organization's outreach. He stated that approximately 12 million books have been distributed from this organization, including books given to 120 foreign countries. Jails, hospitals, prisons, military bases, aircraft carriers, drop-in centers, schools, homeless shelters,

Native American reservations, colleges and a monastery all had profited from the largesse of Irwin Herman and his associates. The Bookman's efforts are much more than lighting one little candle in the darkness; his influence has had a wide impact.

I was amazed that no one had ever written a book about this organization. Occasional articles in the newspaper or appearances on television appeared to me totally inadequate to describe the work of this extensive organization. If such a book had been produced, I would have read it immediately with pleasure. Not only had no one written this book, nor did the prospect of such a book appear on the horizon. Furthermore, I realized that the Bookman would re-retire in all likelihood in 10 or 20 years. Now was the ideal time to describe him and his organization. I felt that the stones might cry out if the whole world did not become aware of this triumph of the human spirit, of this practical embodiment of the ideal. More people should know about what one dreamer can accomplish for the good of humanity.

I felt myself suffering from information overload. Since no book had been written about him and the organization, I found myself wondering whether I dared ask Mr. Herman if I could take on the Bookman and his outfit as a subject for my own book. Having already written five books, I had some awareness of how much commitment is involved in such a project. For several days I juggled the issue in my mind. I worried about a couple of my other projects being shoved to the back burner. I wondered about the time and money involved in writing a book and trying to get it published. I called several of my friends for advice. My colleague Mark seemed to think I should write only one chapter on the Bookman and find other interesting stories of volunteers to fill out a book; nevertheless, he said, "Your enthusiasm will be the deciding factor in the success of this venture." Several others gave me a clear green light to continue. As it turned out I did discover and write briefly about several other local philanthropists in my quest.

Before volunteering to take on the task of showing forth the Bookman and his organization, I began to assess just what writing such a book might entail. There are really two sides to the issue.

The first is to discover and portray all the people and means that made available the millions of books that were constantly being provided for readers around the world. Irwin Herman began talking about all the people who had assisted him in his task. I would need to chronicle just how the gates open for this flood of books let loose on San Diego and the outer world.

The second and more difficult task would be to examine the result of all these efforts. I felt that all those who provided these books were a bit like a small boy putting a message in a bottle and tossing it into the ocean. The boy wonders to what shores the bottle will be washed. He wonders what people may discover when they read the message. It would certainly be impossible to interview all the people who have read these books and have recorded the impact these works have made on them. Even if I should discover everyone who had received one of the Bookman's books and even read them, it would be difficult to assess the impact the book has made on that reader.

With trepidation, I picked up the phone and set up an appointment with the Bookman for lunch to explore the idea of my writing the book in question. He suggested we meet in his office. I insisted on meeting him at a restaurant, knowing that a discussion in a restaurant when one is treating is more likely to bring the desired result than a discussion in an office. My assistant April and I waited outside Coco's restaurant for the Bookman. Since April had never met him and I see poorly since I am legally blind, I worried a bit about identifying him. When he arrived, there was no mistaking the Bookman. For one thing, he greeted me. For another thing, he arrived right on time explaining that he did not practice arriving late for appointments, since to do so is wasting others' time. As soon as the waitress seated us, I presented him with three books I had already written. I wanted him to examine them to see whether he thought I would be a good fit for the project of writing about his organization. I also gave him three references, which he waved away, saying, "I'm from Chicago. We can read a man by looking him in the eye for five minutes, and I've already read you." Apparently I passed the scrutiny. It was obvious to him that I was visually handicapped because I had my mobility cane with me. Both he and I, without words, recognized that it is ability and not disability that counts.

There really is no interviewing this man. It's like opening up a faucet and the information comes out, filling the cup and running over. After we finished eating our sandwiches, April was busy trying to take a few notes about his life. At the age of eight he began selling newspapers for a man who ran a portable news stand. Later he bought the cart and the business for ten dollars. After his father became ill when Herman was 12 years old, he took over the daily running of his father's vacuum cleaner and appliance repair business. At his father's death, when Herman was 16, he took ownership of the business, including his father's debts. He probably could have avoided paying off those debts if he had chosen to, but he visited every person to whom his father owed money, promising to pay them when he was able. That worked out very well for Herman. The creditors were so impressed that they helped him secure loans for the business he had just taken over. Those virtues of accountability and credibility followed him throughout his life.

The waitress interrupted Mr. Herman's talk by asking us whether we wanted dessert. I replied that the doctor, pointing to myself, says no. Mr. Herman was too engrossed in his subject to pause to eat more food. I gathered, too, that he must have watched his diet, since his energetic manner indicated that he didn't sit around eating all the time. Mr. Herman resumed his talk by informing us that after forty years of running the business (it must have been quite successful), he left it to his son who was in need of an income and Herman and his wife retired to San Carlos, California. Rather than enjoying his retirement, he found it boring. He deplored such activities as tagging along after his wife on one of her shopping adventures.

Tom Assad was a friend of Herman's who taught at a local prison and mentioned to him that the prisoners had no books to read and just sat around during their free time. Herman's reaction was to donate his own library to the local San Diego jails. It was these prisoners who started calling him "The Bookman," a name which has stuck ever since. Not stopping with this gift, he began collecting books from other donors until both his garage was stuffed with books and those garages of three of his neighbors also.

At this point, Diane Bell of the *San Diego Union Tribune* wrote an article about the Bookman. The daughter of a local entrepreneur, Jack Grace, read the article and stepped forward to offer three storage units in her Home Handy business, free of charge. Now Herman had six storage spots.

This went on for about a year and one day while Jack Grace was looking around Home Handy, he chanced to run into Irwin Herman. The two hit it off immediately and Grace said, "I have a building on El Cajon Boulevard I just bought and it has some space I can let you use for a while." Within weeks The Bookman's new home was established–still rent-free. "For a while" has become 15 years and The Bookman has become the anchor tenant in the building.

To my delight and amazement, Mr. Herman assured me that I have access to anything in the organization and to contacts outside it. I have noticed that whenever I approach a private citizen or head of an organization for interviews I am immediately welcome. His name is the magic shibboleth or talisman.

I began this chapter referring to the letter from a Job Corps student who complained about the books that the Bookman gave him to read. The end of the story is that Mr. Herman found out from the young man's teacher just what kind of reading the young man would like. He found books on auto mechanics and had them delivered to this young man.

The stacks at The Bookman

CHAPTER 2

A Morning at The Bookman

For variety's sake and for the sake of a sense of immediacy, I have decided to describe a morning at The Bookman's in dramatic form. Indeed, a visit to The Bookman usually results in a little drama. Between the Bookman's comments and his visitors there is usually a little show.

Art: (To assistant, Julie) We're going to the Bookman instead of to my office this morning. Turn right here at 37th Street and take the first driveway on your left.

Julie: There's about 200 feet of brightly colored paintings on the wall alongside the driveway leading up to the Bookman's warehouse. Who painted all of these pictures?

Art: It was the Bookman's idea to give young people a chance to express their creativity. He provided the supplies then let them paint whatever they wanted to paint. I think some of the painters came from the school next door. What do you think of the paintings? What style is the art?

Julie: I'd say it reminds me of Chicano style. It's like getting a shot of encouragement just to look at them.

Art: Find any parking space you can. You'll see the sign directing you to the Bookman's workshop.

Julie: This isn't an imposing sign.

Art: Nor is it an elegant entrance. It looks like what it is—stairs to a warehouse. They haven't made an attempt to disguise it."

(They climb the stairs for a while.)

Art: It seems like we've been climbing a bit too long.

Julie: That's because we've gone too far. Let's go back down a floor. Here it is. I guess we missed the entrance because it's not that obvious when you're climbing up.

(They enter a hallway leading to a larger room.)

Art: Julie, look here at the walls—these are thank you letters the Bookman has received."

Julie: I see a world map with pins all over it.

Art: Those are the places where the Bookman has sent books. He's covered much of the world. (The Bookman is seated at his desk by the phone. Tony the Elf spots Art and Julie.)

Tony: You have visitors, Irwin.

Art: (Offers the gift of coffee to Irwin Herman, the Bookman.) This is my new assistant, Julie Randolph. My former assistant, April Anderson, is doing Ph.D. work at one of the Claremont Colleges.

Bookman: Thank you for the coffee. It's always good to see you. How have you been? Julie, did you get to see any of the thank you notes when you came in?

Julie: I was looking at the map with all the places you've sent books to. You have an amazing amount of books here!

Bookman: I have boxes of those thank you notes. Yes, our object is to give away these books as fast as we can to people who need them. So, how's the book coming? When will I get to read it? Are you going to wait till I die before finishing it?

Art: Our object today is to find letters and identify the people who are reading the books.

Bookman: Don't you already have a lot of people you've interviewed?

Art: Yes, but we need more.

Bookman: Why do you need any more?

Julie: Well, he's a writing teacher so he knows he needs to give lots of examples!

Art: I want to know more about the Native American reservation you sent books to.

Bookman: That was several years ago. Did you ever hear about the pet owner who approached the priest to have a mass said for his dog who had just died? The priest said, "We don't say masses for animals."

"Oh, said the pet owner. I'll just take this $5,000 check down to the rabbi and ask him to do the funeral."

"Hold on!" said the priest. "You didn't tell me the dog was a Catholic!"

(Art and Julie laugh.)

Bookman: (Notices Julie writing on her notepad.) Here's a clipboard with the edge chewed off. It used to belong to a frustrated author.

Art: I thought you'd show Julie that special picture frame you once held in front of your face; the one you showed me. What are you doing collecting toilet seats anyway?

Bookman: I collect various items that help the handicapped. From canes to walkers–even that toilet seat. (The phone rings.)

Bookman: Did you say a school in the Philippines needs books? How many do you need? Yes, you can come by and choose the books. Yes, we have books for children. You'll have to provide the shipping. Stop by any week day during the morning. See you then.

(Turning to Art.) That man needs a boatload of books for a school in the Philippines.

Art: How do the books get to where they're needed?

Bookman: He'll have to rent a cargo container and pay for the shipping, but the books are free. (He sees Julie looking at two letters from the president of Virginia Tech University.) Did I tell you that we created two libraries in honor of Professor Liviu Librescu of Virginia Tech? He's the professor who was killed when he blocked the doorway to his classroom when a gunman went through the campus. This is the kind of life I respect.

(A cheerful middle-aged African American woman, dressed in colors of the rainbow, enters with a 7-year-old boy in tow.)

Bookman: Good morning! How are you, Jamillah and Isaiah?

Jamillah: Isaiah has something he wants to give you.

Bookman: You do? Did you read that book you picked out last time?

Isaiah: Yes.

Jamillah: Oh, he read it all!

Bookman: You want to pick out another one today? Go ahead!

Jamillah: Give Mr. Irwin the card, Isaiah.

Bookman: Jamillah, this is Art Seamans and his assistant, Julie. Art is writing a book about what we do here. (He reads the card.) I'd like to show this to Art and Julie.

Art: Julie, read the card to me.

Julie: It's such a nice card. Someone decorated it with a boy and a girl, a sun and books–and here's another girl on roller skates holding a lollipop. Did you make this, Isaiah? (He nods.) Good job! Inside it says, "Many thanks from the New Heritage Church." Other people have signed it and someone wrote, "The first time I ever write these words I ever thought is that you guys are the happiest book group I ever found out." That's a heartfelt endorsement, isn't it?

Art: What do you do with the books you get from the Bookman?

Jamillah: Last time we picked up books for the Heritage Weekend Celebration Banquet at the New Heritage Church. I work with the youth there. I'm looking for books for kids' science workshops at the Marketplace.

(Isaiah returns with six books.)

Bookman: Did you find some good ones, young man?

Jamillah: Isaiah, isn't that too many books?

Bookman: No, as long as he promises to read them. You will, won't you Isaiah?

Isaiah: I'll read them all.

Jamillah: He's quite a reader, so he probably will.

(They leave.)

Bookman: We meet some of the best people in town. Did you hear about Isaac Finkelstein and the wonderful garments he sewed? One day Jesus came by and saw his wonderful work and asked him to make a robe. The robe looked terrific and Jesus was pleased enough to offer to help Isaac with his business. They argued about what to call their new venture, finally settling on Lord and Taylor.

(The elevator hums and on it appears a woman with boxes and boxes of books.)

Woman: Good morning! This time I'm bringing books rather than taking them. My employer recently died and left about 500 books. A lot of these books are on psychology. I was tempted to give them to my college library but I want these books to help people, so I brought them here.

Bookman: We'll take them off your hands.

(The elves help the woman bring the books into the warehouse from the freight elevator.)

Julie: I like this photo of you with the Olympic torch in 1996.

Bookman: I was a lot younger then. I ran down Park Boulevard from Balboa Park for about a mile. I still have the torch. That was quite an honor. Did you ever hear about the drunk Irishman at the wake?

(Art and Julie laugh.)

(At about 10:00 a.m. a woman enters with two young men. Art is seated in a chair near the Bookman's desk as the Bookman fields questions on the telephone.)

Woman: (Seeing the Bookman is on the phone, she speaks to Art instead.) Do you know the Bookman?

Art: I'd better know him–I'm writing a book on him!

Julie: We'd like to ask you some questions about the Bookman for the book.

Woman: I'm Betty Lopez. I work at Southwest Key. It's a residential program that helps undocumented youth here in San Diego. I have two of our clients here with me today. Our clients are provided by I.C.E., U.S. Immigration and Customs Enforcement. Southwest Key is a recognized leader in design and implementation of innovative, community-based youth justice programs for federal, state and local agencies. We provide a less expensive and more supportive environment than detention in the youth justice system.

Art: I've never heard of that organization.

Betty: We've been around for a while. The young men with me today are being rewarded for good behavior by a trip to the Bookman today. They refused to run away when two of our other residents escaped and tried to lead the group to do the same.

Art: May I interview the boys?

Betty: I'll have to interpret for you. Neither of them speaks much English yet.

The teens have gone to rear of an aisle and are intently examining books written in Spanish. Art introduces himself and both boys shake hands with him like adults.

Art: Where did you learn to read?

Teen #1: I learned to read in school in my home country.

Teen #2: I'm learning how to read in this program.

Art: What kind of books do you like?

Teen #1: Stories and history.

Teen #2: The same for me.

Betty: You're welcome to visit the farm where the youth live.

Art: You have a farm?

Betty: Well, that's what we call it. We have some animals and a garden. The boys learn and they do chores to help them gain work skills.

(They return to selecting books for Southwest Key and for themselves.)

Bookman: I'm going to have to wrap things up here. I need to meet my wife at the nursing home for lunch.

Art: Well, we have plenty of material at this point. It's good to see you again. Enjoy lunch with your wife.

Julie: Thank you so much for your time and for letting me go through your thank you letters again.

Bookman: Not at all. We'll see you again.

Art: Julie, let's stop at Johnny R's for lunch and we'll go over your notes.

(Art and Julie return to the car. On the way to the restaurant they talk about the morning's adventure.)

Art: How in the world would these two scared rabbits be able to find their way in this country without knowing English and without any adult supervision? How would they survive and what would happen to them? How little do we realize the situations some people are in! When I think of how fortunate some of us are and how desperately impoverished others are and how little I am aware of the existence of these needy people, I am ashamed. Does my lack of awareness excuse me from helping these needy people? How can we wake up to what's going on right around us? Thank God there are people like Betty and organizations like Southwest Key to provide guidance to young people like those two.

Julie: Maybe we can make a donation. We'll add them to the list.

(At Johnny R's, Art waxes philosophical over chili and grilled cheese sandwiches.)

Art: Ideas have consequences. Your thoughts, your beliefs, your philosophy, your faith have consequences in this world. I know we all have weaknesses and are not perfect, but I just can't understand how people who hurt others by robbing or defrauding them, or even by being indifferent to them, can live with themselves. Have they no fear of the Judgment or even the judgment of themselves when they look in the mirror?

Julie: It's very easy to miss the point of life in all the details and struggles of daily living, but if you think of every good, beautiful, and true thing you've ever experienced, it can lead you back in the right direction. Prayer and reflection are an important part of remembering goodness, beauty and truth.

Art: Of course, but I would add that the humanities, the study of literature, philosophy, history and the arts help to create citizens who are responsible and caring. I am alarmed that only 1% of college graduates are English majors. I know Garrison Keillor and others joke about them, but we need them and many more of them. Fortunately, there are many elementary and high school teachers who are also working these humanistic disciplines into their teaching.

Julie: Absolutely. I was one of those English majors.

Art: And that's why you're so caring.

The world suddenly seems brighter as they finish lunch and read the many thank you notes written to The Bookman organization.

Art: (Sighs) Dr. Johnson said a chair at a pub is the throne of human felicity.

Julie: Or a booth at Johnny R's.

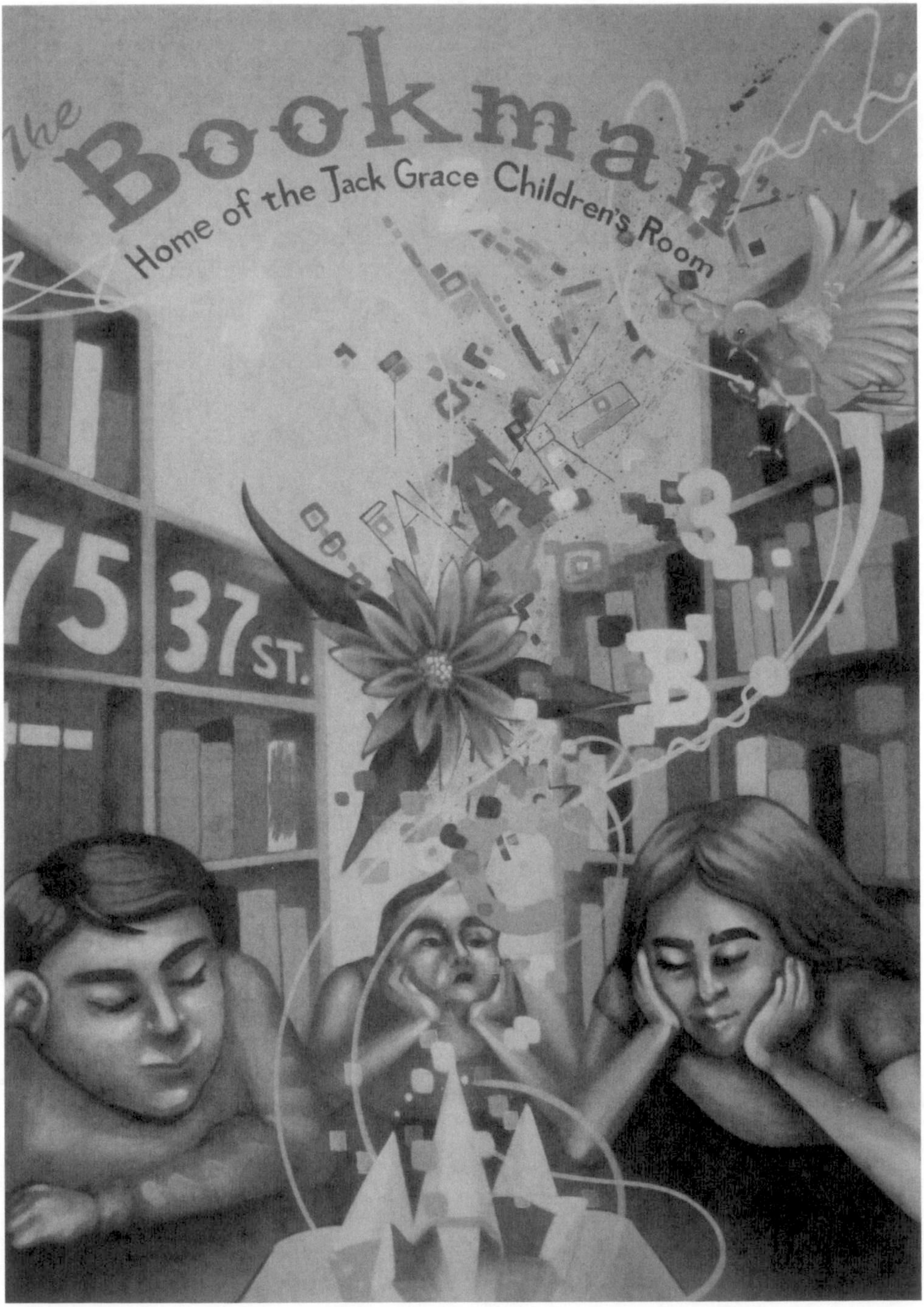
The Bookman
Home of the Jack Grace Children's Room
75
37 ST.

CHAPTER 3

Love of Books

Occasionally former students and their friends meet at my condo to discuss our current writing. When my turn came to read, I read from my in-progress writing on "The Bookman." I was reading my description of the Bookman to a small group when one of the listeners surprised me by saying, "We understand about the Bookman's love of books, but how did you acquire a love of books? Why are you so fascinated with the Bookman's attempt to distribute these books to all who want them?" I suppose I take it for granted that everyone sees the importance of books and loves to read them. I didn't suppose that I was unique in treasuring the printed word. When I was asked the question, "Why do you love books?" I realized that an explanation of the reason was forthcoming. I had intended to leave myself out of this account of the Bookman and his organization. After all, I had already written a memoir about myself. I had intended just to be the chronicler of the Bookman and his efforts. It seemed probable, however, that I could not fail to include myself. Without the fire in my belly and in the Bookman's belly there would be no dynamo to this book.

I don't believe I'd ever had the question about the roots of my interest in the Bookman's organization asked quite that way, nor have I had anyone ask me about the source of my love for books. The question forced me to go back and dig around my life. Such digging is useful if one is to understand what motivates oneself. To describe my love for books and the role they have played in my life is like asking a plant to describe its growth by listing all the occasions on which it received rain and sun and nutriment from the soil. I remember searching for pivotal points in my growth as it was furthered by reading books. I didn't like school at all until I got to high school except for Mrs. McCarthy's third grade class. She read Frances Hodgson Burnett's *The Secret Garden*. How I looked forward to those classes when she would read to us from what was for me a marvelous book.

Before *The Secret Garden* the only literary work I remember, apart from the Bible, was the Dick and Jane series. One of the episodes in the Dick and Jane saga was situated in Dick and Jane's house. My older brothers picked up one of my books and laughed because Jane could not find Dick, who was hiding behind a door. Finally, Dick pushed open the door and announced, "Here I am, Jane! You have found me in the house." My brothers taunted me with the logic of that statement. Jane had not found Dick; he had revealed his location to her. Don't blame me, I thought. I didn't write the book.

The account of the children's playing with Spot pales in comparison to the story we were reading in Sunday school in which snakes were biting the children of Israel in the desert. I did not appreciate the dumbing down I was getting in elementary school, nor did I appreciate the dumbing down I got in children's church. Some stern spinster, her hair tied behind her head in a knot, explained black hearts and white hearts to us. In fact, she illustrated the concept. She produced a glass of black water. She then dropped a pill into the glass which changed the black water to white water. The pill, she indicated, was symbolic of God's grace. I contrasted the spinster's talk about black and white hearts with the expository sermons about sin and redemption in the Pauline epistles heard in the adult services.

At the sixth grade I advanced my secular reading from Dick and Jane and became addicted to the Western novels of Zane Grey. Here was a world of high adventure quite different from the mundanity of my everyday life. I was also intrigued by books on Alaska. They pictured a world far away from the world in which I was planted. In Alaska one only battled against the elements, not against the tyranny of peer pressure in school.

In my freshman year of high school, we were assigned Sir Walter Scott's *Ivanhoe*. Ye high school teachers, avoid Scott and Ivanhoe for your freshman readers! In my senior year, we read MacBeth and snippets from the great poets, but I don't recall being excited or challenged about my reading then. At college I became enamored of writers like Keats, Shelley, Wordsworth and Arnold. One usually can't get into an author's thought with just one poem. Shelley's "The Cloud" is a wonderfully descriptive poem, but does not carry the central message of the author's writing. While I read some books in high school, I was not really turned on to books. Incidentally, most of the homeless people I have been interviewing do not attribute their love of reading to their experiences in school either.

All my life I had looked forward to college, largely because I'd heard about all the fun that was to be had there. Since I had imaged college as social activity I was a bit shocked in orientation week when I had to purchase textbooks for the fall. Hadn't I been through with school books when I graduated from high school? I'm talking here about my feelings, not any logic. The first week of classes changed my whole attitude toward textbooks and learning. I began to look forward to classes and the books I was assigned to read. As one of my reading assignments I decided to read *Leaves of Grass* by Walt Whitman. He gave me a glimpse of a world not regulated by the puritanical ideas that had surrounded me in my childhood. We also read Rollvaag's *Giants in the Earth*. My excitement about reading serious literature was beginning. In my sophomore year, I was introduced to Henry David Thoreau's *Walden* and Mark Twain's *Huckleberry Finn*. Somehow, I resonated with these books and realized that I was not some weird exception to everybody else. These good writers did not moralize or sweeten their picture of life. My literature teacher, Bertha Munro, maintained that books that fail to reveal what life is really like are more reprehensible than books like *Lady Chatterley's Lover*, a book once banned in libraries.

I'm not sure it was a great compliment but my American Literature teacher called me a second Huckleberry Finn because of my careless appearance and rebellious thinking. It's true I bought a pair of new pants and cuffed them with pins because I didn't want to bother with taking them to the tailor. This act did not endear me to the ladies in my classes. My sister, who was a senior, was scandalized because I wore a dark cloth shirt over my white shirt instead of a sport coat at church one Sunday morning. Of course, now it's called the layered look.

When I entered college I thought I might enter the ministry because so much of my life growing up revolved around church and church activities. A senior said to me, "Art, are you planning to go to seminary?" When I responded affirmatively he said, "You'd be better off majoring in a liberal arts course than in theology. You'll get lots of Bible and theology in seminary." At the end of my sophomore year, I was talking casually with some of my dorm mates. Suddenly someone asked me, "What are you majoring in, Art?" Without thinking I said, "English." Immediately something told me that was the right fit for me. When I began my junior year in my major I became something of a fanatic. I was astounded at how many writers spoke to me meaningfully about my life and experiences. I had the sensation of thousands of hands reaching out to me in the darkness of my mental isolation. The more I read, the more excited I became. It didn't take me long to decide that my life's work would be to share my enthusiasm, my treasure, with others.

My enthusiasm for books carried me through work on my master's and doctor's degrees, both studies immensely enjoyable. However, in spite of all my formal studies, I realized that improving one's reading and becoming acquainted with the world's literature is a lifelong process. The more one reads the more one realizes how little one has read and how much there is out there begging to be read. I tell my students that reading well is like dancing well; it takes two to tango. I assert that there is little doubt that the writers in their textbooks know how to dance. The challenge is for them to cultivate their skills in reading so that they will be up to the dance with these wonderful partners.

Apart from my formal training, I was fortunate to have two models to challenge me in my reading. While I was working on my Ph.D. at the University of Maryland and teaching at Columbian Preparatory School, I met Jack Dagiliatus. He reminded me of the Old Testament character Melchizedek. I had no idea of Jack's background, nor did he reveal it, nor any concept of his future plans. He seemed to have come from nowhere and disappeared like the mists of the morning. I would say he was about 30 years old, very aristocratic in appearance and dress. He possessed the power to fascinate students in the class. The classes he taught often ran as many as 20 minutes over time with no apparent restlessness from the students. It was a little frustrating trying to begin class in the room that he had not vacated.

In an endeavor to persuade me to include *The Brothers Karamazov* in our curriculum, he took me one evening at dusk into the headmaster's office, empty at the time, and read me the Grand Inquisitor chapter. All the mystic ambience of the novel seeped into my consciousness in the dusk of that room. Jack persistently needled me on my reading practice. Every day he asked, "What are you reading now?" If the truth be told, I was busy reading for my graduate classes and had little time for current books. He encouraged me to go with him to visit the poet Ezra Pound who at the time was incarcerated in St. Elizabeth's Hospital. Since I had read little of Pound's writing and cared less for it, I declined the offer. He also invited me to a session where T.S. Eliot would read his poetry and comment on it. How I have regretted that I did not take him up on the offer!

Where now, bright spirit, art thou? I can't find him on the internet. He may now be in Nepal or Zanzibar, fascinating all who meet him. I vowed, however, that once I was through with my graduate studies I would read, I hoped, as much as a book a day. Have I kept that vow? No, alas! But I try.

The second motivational reader taught with me at a prep school in Maine. Bob Brown was a graduate of Oxford University and had received a masters degree from Cambridge University. Bob was teaching at Albany State during the year and appeared at the Winter Harbor Reading School in the summer. There I taught with him. In fact, my classroom was next to his. He claimed to have read 200 novels a year. It was worth going to St. Christopher's by the Sea on Sunday to hear him perform as the lay reader of the lesson. Bob Brown resembled a middle-aged headmaster, or perhaps a priest. His rounded features were set in contrast to the sharpness of his intellect and the precision of his language. One afternoon, in the empty classroom, I played a record of Stephen Crane's story *An Episode of War.* I was not aware that Brown was listening from his bedroom upstairs. I could hear him move as softly and reverently as if he were walking up the aisle in a church processional. Then he exclaimed with awe over a phrase heard on the record–"The mystery of a bullet's journey."

Brown constantly bombarded me with great novels he had read. Every summer he came with a different poem that he would announce as "the poem of the year." He would neither explain his choice of the poem nor explicate it. One year he came with this poem by Emily Dickinson that he declared was the greatest poem in the English language:

> I asked no other thing,
> No other was denied.
> I offered Being for it;
> The mighty merchant smiled.
> Brazil? He twirled a button,
> Without a glance my way:
> "But, madam, is there nothing else
> That we can show to-day?"

He explained that brazil was a kind of cloth.

He insisted that I read *Pale Fire* by Vladimir Nabokov. I was frustrated reading that book until the last chapter when everything marvelously came together. Brown was right in recommending the book. He recommended a number of books that I have enjoyed. After four years Brown did not return to Maine for summer school. Instead he headed north to somewhere near the Arctic Circle, the University of Oulu in Finland.

As I talked to Irwin Herman at his book establishment on El Cajon Boulevard, I realized that he, too, like Jack and Bob, developed a love of reading quite apart from school assignments. I shared his view that before us was a treasure that needed not to be hoarded but to be shared. What drives Irwin Herman is that same impulse that drives me. No caring human being can stand by while he sees another human being starve. No person who has experienced the wonder, wisdom, and life that come from reading can rest at peace when he becomes aware that there are vast sections of humanity that have no ready access to books, although tens of thousands of new books are published every year in the United States alone. To think of the mental starvation the Bookman heard about in jails and prisons contrasted with the fantastic abundance and wealth of printed books seems intolerable to the Bookman and to me. How to bring this food to the starving is the Bookman's challenge. It is my challenge to write about how he performs this deed.

Jack Grace

CHAPTER 4

Jack Grace

To found an organization with as wide a sweep as the Bookman's requires a leader who can inspire others with his dream. An essential quality of Irwin Herman is that ability to inspire and enlist others in his cause. No more important follower has appeared on the scene in support of the Bookman's enterprise than Jack Grace, whom the Bookman dubbed Jack "Amazing" Grace. As I picked up the notes to write about Jack Grace, I received the shocking news that he had passed away. A person's death gives others the freedom to praise his life, knowing that the object of one's praise cannot influence what one says about him. Death puts the seal on a person's life and so I can speak of Jack Grace without any hesitancy that what I say might be flattery.

I can freely express my admiration for the accomplishments and the character of this man whom I met through my pursuit of this book. I quickly realized that Jack Grace was so naturally and comfortably who he was that he put those who approached him completely at ease. So when I called him and identified myself as a person who wished to write a book on the Bookman, Jack Grace was completely accommodating. No, I did not need to take him to a restaurant. He lived near the campus of Point Loma Nazarene University and therefore was glad to meet me on campus. The coffee shop would be a fine place to talk. I worried about how I would identify him as he came on campus. I need not have. He called out my name as I approached the parking lot and we proceeded to the coffee shop on campus for the interview. Jack, like all the others, seemed absolutely open to my questions. He was neither defensive nor concerned about my qualifications for writing this book.

As we sat drinking coffee I asked how he had met the Bookman. He responded, "It was through my daughter, whom I had appointed manager of the old Bekins Moving and Storage building where the Bookman's warehouse is now located." Mr. Grace told me that Irwin Herman had approached his daughter with the idea of renting a room or two for The Bookman operation, preferably on the first floor. When his daughter apprised him of this request, Jack Grace decided to discover just what was behind it. Why did this man want to have a place to store thousands of used books? The more he found out about The Bookman organization, the more he admired both its founder and the aims of the operation. Irwin Herman reported that whenever Jack Grace visited the warehouse he had a satisfied smile on his face. Grace liked that The Bookman was a charity with no overhead. Anything that was given was passed immediately to the purpose of the organization. None of the helpers received a salary of any kind, nor did Mr. Herman. In fact, Mr. Herman put some of his own finances into running it. Here was a charity that Mr. Grace could identify with and support without fear of wasting his money. And so, suggesting to the Bookman that he take the second floor, Jack Grace gave him the keys to the space.

I said, "Yes, the Bookman tells me that not only do you provide him with space rent free but you also supply heat and light in addition to other donations." Mr. Grace admitted nonchalantly that it was so. As we sat drinking coffee, I could not help wondering whether the meeting of Jack Grace with Irwin Herman was just serendipitous. How was it that in seeking a place to rent, Irwin Herman could run into this able and charitable man? Students poured into the coffee shop at this juncture and their noise plus the omnipresent television encouraged us to seek a quieter refuge. We left the coffee house to go to the lounge in the Literature department. As we sat down, I noticed that Mr. Grace carried a packet with him. He opened it, pulled out its contents and handed them to me.

With a bit of a shock I heard him say, "I have all the newspaper clippings about The Bookman and all the financial statements about the organization for your inspection."

With amazement I asked, "Are these your only copies?" Would he entrust this file to someone he'd just met? Yes, they were his only copies. I promised to return them as soon as my assistant could copy them.

As we continued to talk, Jack Grace volunteered further reasons for why he supported the Bookman's organization. "It is better," he said, "to give a fishing pole to the needy than to give them a fish." He saw books as a means of helping people to help themselves. I was a bit amused by his comment that the motivation for Irwin Herman's commitment to the project escaped him. I could ask the same question of Jack Grace. He underlined the opinion of Don that Herman is primarily a people person. One of the mysteries of the operation is the loyalty he commands from the three elves. The only thing Herman gives them is a cheap lunch every day.

I inquired a bit about the history of the life of the man sitting opposite me. He replied with some information. Jack grew up in a number of places since his father was an officer in the Army. It is understandable that he then sought admission to West Point, attending the Sullivan School in preparation for entrance. It triggered my own memories of teaching at such a school–the Columbian Preparatory School, which was about a mile from the Sullivan School in Washington, D.C. Both the Sullivan School and Columbian Preparatory School were year-long schools, the purpose of both being to raise the scores of those wishing to enter one of the service academies. I have very warm memories of teaching at Columbian Preparatory School; so I felt some bond with Jack Grace, who had been a student at one of them. His attendance at West Point and his career as an officer in the Army helped explain his tall, dignified, rather military bearing. He also informed me that he and his companion both played tennis, sometimes on this very campus. At West Point he studied electrical engineering and thus became involved in working on short-range missiles. In fact, he operated a nuclear silo at one time. I ventured that such a responsibility was quite exciting. He did not think so. After working for several engineering companies he invested money in construction work. This investment led him to the owning of certain apartment buildings. Having decided to leave the ownership of apartment buildings, he saw the burgeoning need for storage facilities and began purchasing them. Grace had a relaxed, easy manner, possessing a subtle sense of humor. He commented that most people can't bear to get rid of their junk. They put it in storage for nine months and then abandon it.

His name was Grace. Everything about him suggested that quality. He invited me to his house for drinks. Before driving to his house in his Prius, of which he was a proud owner, we toured the campus. It had been several years since he had been on the campus to play tennis. His home seemed to be a typical, comfortable Point Loma home with a front porch and a large outdoor space in the back which used to be a swimming pool and had been filled in to make a practice putting range. I would have preferred the pool. Once inside he introduced me to Cathy, who sat in an easy chair with her sixteen-year-old calico cat. I could not lure the cat to me to get its fur patted. I got the impression of the Graces as being people with huge inner character and energy hidden by a quiet, serene, and dignified exterior. They sat, drinking wine, while I had to ask for juice since I'm a teetotaler. Although I'd spoken with him a couple of times on the telephone, this meeting was my only personal contact with him. In retrospect, I can say that he was one of the few older men whom I admire without reservation. His generosity, his friendliness, his openness, his sense of humor reminded me of a Mr. Harold Tynor whom I knew as a child. I resolved as a youth that when I became a little older I would be like Mr. Tynor. Now I resolve that I would like to have the virtues exhibited by Mr. Jack Grace.

The Elves: Irwin Herman, Darryl (a friend), Leonard, Tony and Don

CHAPTER 5

The Elves

The three dedicated volunteers who help run the warehouse are called the elves. Like the late Jack Grace and like Ron Blair, from The Nice Guys whom we shall discuss later, these crucial helpers prefer to keep a low profile.

My first interview was with Lenny the Elf. I had first suggested that we take each elf out separately for lunch. They vetoed the idea since it would intrude on their common lunch with the Bookman. Lenny took out a key and we entered Irwin Herman's private office, the inner sanctum. I was led to believe that it was a high privilege to enter this room. I expected some plush suite with kitchenette and lounge chairs and dancing women. Alas, it had very little more elegance than the warehouse itself. There were pictures of Irwin Herman's family and–perhaps his most prized possession–Indian feathers given to him by an Indian reservation for which he had provided books. These feathers represent the highest honor that the reservation could bestow upon the Bookman. In addition to the eagle feathers in the office there were the dream catchers. I had not seen or heard of them before. They look like spider webs, and I am told they catch bad dreams. I could see nothing else that needed to be protected. There were teapots and candlesticks on top of the bookshelves, teddy bears on a chair, Asian dolls, and family photos around the room. The cement floor was covered by an unremarkable throw rug. The place was loaded with books; in fact, I couldn't put my feet under the desk to write because something was under there–solid and immovable. In any case, I was honored to be invited into the room, since they considered it an honor. There was no coffee there or snacks or any of the other amenities of life.

As I recall, there were some high windows near the ceiling. I could've suggested remodeling the place but apparently my advice was not needed nor welcomed. I have to remember that some people don't like the décor in my condominium. When I showed my condominium to my colleague Mike McKinney, he did not say, "You have an attractive condominium," he simply said, "It looks like you." If that isn't an ambiguous statement, I've never heard one.

As I have indicated before, the Bookman has the rare gift of inspiring others to work with him. Such a gift was possessed by Mark Twain's Tom Sawyer. You will recall that one nice summer day Aunt Polly insisted that Tom Sawyer whitewash the fence before he could have some adventures with his friends. When some of these friends dropped by, taunting him with the fact that they were free while Tom had to work, Tom resorted to a strategy. He acted as if whitewashing that fence was the most fun thing imaginable. He dipped the brush into the whitewash and swung it towards the boards with great panache. Now, activity is more fascinating than inactivity. What red blooded boy wants to stand and watch someone else do whatever someone else is doing? When Tom expressed no interest in abandoning the project to pursue some other activity, one of his friends asked if he could try his hand at whitewashing the fence for a while. Tom treated the request as a favor to be granted. After some hesitation he let each boy take his hand at whitewashing the fence for a fee. Thus, the work of whitewashing the entire fence quickly was accomplished.

My Uncle Foster had some of the charisma of a Tom Sawyer. All through my high school years I would hitchhike up to the town of Adams Center, New York partly to work on my Uncle Foster's milk route and in his carpentry shop where he built rowboats. Everybody seemed to want to work for my Uncle Foster. A local man, named Francis, and a young man from the church who my Uncle nicknamed Speedy (for ironical reasons) were some of the devoted workers whom my uncle enlisted. Certainly the Bookman possesses this charisma. He is ready to give tribute to the three "elves", retired men who donate almost full-time work without compensation to The Bookman organization. When you visit the warehouse on El Cajon Boulevard these men remain in the background, rushing around the warehouse busy with their tasks. They are a bit like bees in a beehive. I know the beehive is a cliché but it fits. They even seem averse to being interviewed since such an interview would interrupt their work. I got the impression that they somewhat resented being invaded by a person off the streets. Who was I to barge in, asking questions about them and their organization?

Like all of the four men there, Lenny, or formally, Leonard Pearlman, once had a business career as a salesman and manager with Sears. Like all of the men there, he worked hard. Lenny revealed that his wife of many years had died two years previously, but he had three living daughters. Through Lenny's wife he met the Bookman. I bluntly asked how old he was, admitting I was seventy-nine. He confessed to being a year younger but he seemed more vigorous than I am. I found out that Leonard paid special attention to the children's section.

After Leonard left, he sent Don Schulz into the inner sanctum for the interview. Don is the youngest of the gang of four, and in one sense has had the most relevant background in handling used books since he ran two used bookstores in San Diego. One catered to romances for women readers. Don uses this background to help him organize the stacks of books. He reports that Irwin often will set the books he receives and other material down on shelves–so preoccupied is he with meeting the public. As a used bookstore owner Don had the necessity to develop the ability to evaluate the worth of books to particular reader audiences. Don takes pride in keeping the place organized. His knowledge of books also evidences itself with his work alongside the third volunteer, Tony, who assesses the monetary value of books. Such things as first editions or rare copies can be sold for money to help the organization. Don's knowledge of used books helps also in weeding out books that are inappropriate or possessing little value.

Don gave me an interesting account of a boy who asked for work at one of his bookstores. He paid the boy a dollar an hour. Two things grew out of this venture: he became a kind of foster father to the boy. Recently Don visited him in Germany where he is stationed as an officer in the Army and is rearing children of his own. The second outcome of this venture is the romance that developed between the boy's mother and himself.

I was a bit amused when Don mentioned Scientology. Since I know very little about Scientology it is well that I made no comment about it, especially a negative comment, since Don revealed himself as a Scientologist. I assumed that he is proud of the fact and wants the world to know this about himself. Of course, I didn't ask any of them about their religious affiliation, though Irwin and Leonard both mentioned their Jewish heritage. Really, their religious affiliation is of little relevance to their work in the organization.

Meeting and talking with people was one of the aspects of running a used bookstore that appealed strongly to Don. He still enjoys meeting people through his volunteer work at the Bookman's organization.

A week later I visited The Bookman establishment again to speak with the heir apparent, Tony Ross. I suppose that Tony, who earned his MBA at the York University in Toronto, has wide experience in heading organizations. In fact, finally, I said to him, "I can't write down everything you have done. There's too much here! Hand me a vita." Suffice it to say that Tony has worked with several publishing organizations, editing, publishing, and marketing many scientific and business journals and books.

Like most Canadians, he was the most matter-of-fact of the group, tossing off his many positions as mere facts. Tony is the one elf on the executive board, which also includes Irwin Herman, Herman's wife, and formerly Jack Grace.

It was through his second wife that Tony arrived in San Diego. He met Irwin while doing volunteer work for The Toussaint Center, a school for homeless teens in downtown San Diego. Since they shared an eagerness to help those who need help, he promised to come back and volunteer at The Bookman after he retired, which he did in 2004.

It appears that the three elves have found an excellent way to spend their retirement, making it enjoyable and fulfilling. Nevertheless, the long-term commitment that these men have made evidences some kind of unusual character and altruism. I wonder also at the seeming lack of friction as they work under Herman and close together with one another. It seems difficult to imagine that the operation could do without them. Jack Grace, Leonard, Don and Tony form some kind of central core of the organization.

I've often wondered about the American structure of labor. We are not allowed to hold much of a job before the age of 18. Between the age of 18 and 65 we labor like ants—or bees. After age 70 we find that our labor is no longer required or usually welcomed. Leonard, Don and Tony would grace any work place, regardless of the age of the other employees.

Over a year later, Julie and I arrived at the Bookman only to be informed by Don that the Bookman was ill that day. This time Don was much more relaxed and even welcomed being interviewed. We found out that his adopted son had advanced to the rank of colonel. He also shared some information about his fellow elves.

Julie asked for more particulars about the bookstores Don had owned. The first store, San Diego Book Exchange, was located on 70th Street and El Cajon Boulevard. He opened the store in 1977 and noted that at that time there were about 50 bookstores in San Diego. When he closed it in 1997 there were only about 20 bookstores left. He also owned Romance World on Main Street in El Cajon. He said that the store carried far more titles in the romance category than a typical bookstore normally held. One day a Southern belle type visited the store, surveyed the walls filled with Silhouette Romances and other notable romance series, and exclaimed, "Why, I'm in hog heaven!" When we asked him if he missed the stores he said, "No, not the stores--I miss the people!" A bookstore owner is somewhat like a bartender, hearing the stories that people tell of their heartbreaks and other adventures. Don said, "I was the corner store and the people were part of the family,"

I told him that I wished to ask some questions about his fellow workers. I was looking for some personal characteristics that would identify them as people. He started with Lenny, noting that Lenny reads books aloud to others many afternoons at a Jewish elementary school. His short hair and white beard make him look like a kindly grandfather. The children call him "Zadie," which means grandfather in Hebrew. Leonard seems to be more playful in working with the books, not as intent on organizing them and moving on. It seems to the others at times that Leonard may still be handling the same book while they are rushing ahead to finish in case another pallet of donated books arrives. Leonard handles the children's books section.

Tony seems to be busy and hurried all the time, quickly accomplishing any task that he sees. Sometimes he and Irwin Herman have a bit of divergence in their strategies. Irwin will put a book on any flat surface --"Even if it's not particularly flat!" Don laughs. Herman is not as concerned with neatness and order as are the others. We noticed that Tony was buzzing around, not stopping to talk with us until we hailed him. Illustrating his efficiency, Don noted that their website popularity soared after Tony took it over, and that the sending of books that they sell online through Alibris had become highly appreciated by customers. Don wishes that Tony would slow down so he can train Don himself fully in the mail order process, which is fairly complicated when dealing with the postal service's ever-changing requirements. Don would like to be more of a jack-of-all-trades around the Bookman's enterprise so that if one person needs to be absent, he can carry out their duties. Don reports that Tony supervises the work of selling books that are of somewhat higher value. All book sales support The Bookman organization and do not go into the pockets of any individual. Three pallets of books arrived recently from a college textbook resale company. About one third of the books were so badly damaged that they had to be destroyed, a third were able to be sold to benefit the Bookman organization, and another third they were able to donate to San Diego City College for student use.

I asked Don what magic power the Bookman has to inspire people to work for him as volunteers. He said it isn't so much Irwin Herman as it is the great challenge of book distribution to those in need that inspires him. He says Herman's days in Chicago taught him his people smarts. "Irwin *shmies* people-- that's a Hebrew word," Don smiles. "Sometimes he'll pull out a stack of books on a topic that a visitor says he likes and then he'll leave it there for them to pick up. We'll come by and ask him if we should put them away and he'll say, 'No! I'm leaving the books there for so-and-so who likes these.'"

I would like to have gotten more, but the elves are too busy to spin tails about their lives.

The Nice Guys, pictured here at one of their fundraisers
for The Bookman, are strong supporters of the operation.

Background, far left and far right:
Shirley Herman (the Bookman's wife), Jack Grace

Foreground, left to right: Bill and Lynelle Lynch, Ron Blair,
Mr. and Mrs. Bob Bradley

CHAPTER 6

Are You a Nice Guy?

There is an organization of businessmen who, like Jack Grace, try to give a helping hand to those in need. It reminds me of the old song, "Each day I'll do a golden deed by helping those who are in need." Like the late Mr. Grace, these people keep a low profile. They heed Henry David Thoreau's advice–"Rescue the perishing and tie your shoestrings."

Irwin Herman told me that a teacher friend of his, Kurt McCarty, whom he met while delivering books to San Diego City College, asked about operations at The Bookman. Herman shared with McCarty some of the needs of the charity. When McCarty heard that Herman needed money to keep things running, he immediately opened his wallet and took out a folded $50 bill from within. "Let me be the first to support you," McCarty said. He also gave Herman the name of John Carlson, a member of The Nice Guys group. Carlson took Herman to lunch at Mr. A's restaurant, a longtime favorite among local restaurants, and the two discussed the most immediate needs of Herman's venture. The van used to deliver books was in need of repair so through the efforts of Nice Guy's contact, Penny White, repairs were facilitated and new tires provided at Drew Ford. Tony Drew himself made sure there was no charge to Herman.

Since these early days in The Bookman's history, the van has been replaced a few times by The Nice Guys. Once, when The Nice Guys heard that his van had been stolen, they provided him with a new one without being asked. When a reporter covering a story about The Bookman wrote that "some nice guys" replaced The Bookman's van, the term "nice guys" stuck.

The Nice Guys have supplied The Bookman with necessary funds to run the operation through their regular fundraisers. Herman indicates that the banquet-style fundraisers take place at local restaurants and he especially remembers a past event at Maitre D's in La Jolla for its elegance. Another favorite memory of Herman's is the banquet where he was recognized along with singer Frankie Lane. The Nice Guys aid The Bookman's efforts in distributing books to the needy at an annual Christmas party they hold at Qualcomm Stadium. It really is difficult to find out who leads the group but I received several names and called one—Ron Blair.

Our daily experiences are like segments of cloth in a patchwork quilt. Sometimes these experiences complement one another; sometimes these experiences contrast with others. As I walked out the door of my condo headed for Coco's restaurant to meet Mr. Ron Blair, my mind was preoccupied with the history book I was in the process of reading. The book details the experiences of Germany in the last days of WWII and the first days after the war ended. The account is largely a horror story of displacement, thefts, hunger, rapes and murders which abounded in this terrible period of Germany's history. Almost every country, including Germany itself, and far too many persons contributed to the agonies that the German people faced, deserved though some of them may have been. What man will do to man! In times of crisis, humanity throws off its robe of civilization and stoops to barbarism.

As we sat over breakfast, Mr. Ron Blair, described as a key figure in The Nice Guys collective, proceeded to detail a marvelous account of what one group of citizens can accomplish for the betterment of their fellow citizens. The activities of the Nice Guys stand in contrast to the horror stories I had been reading. I thought of the words of the poet Shelley, who wondered—"Such gloom, why man has such a scope/For love and hate, despondency and hope." Opposite me was an unprepossessing man, representative of 150 men and women in The Nice Guys volunteer non-profit organization, who laid out before me a wonderful story of the good that man can do to man. As I left the restaurant, I could not help asking the clerk behind the cash register, "Do you know whom I have been interviewing?" I felt like blowing a trumpet to hail the accomplishments of The Nice Guys.

Irwin Herman had already mentioned the generosity of The Nice Guys to The Bookman enterprise. Before pursuing that connection, I needed to ask Ron Blair some background information about himself and The Nice Guys organization. Mr. Blair informed me that he grew up in California and studied engineering in college. He was drafted out of his program in 1953, a date I, too, remember, since I also was drafted in 1953. His engineering studies led him to found eventually, with a partner, an aerospace production company in San Diego. Some of his fellow businessmen and military men became involved in the Arc of San Diego, an organization which provides help for people with disabilities. Some 30 members of this group decided to form their own organization with a different focus. The spark for their new change of focus was provided by the family of Chad Greene, a young man afflicted with leukemia. In 1979, this family arrived in San Diego to seek a cancer cure. The group of businessmen heard that the family had exhausted its resources and stood desperately in need of help. After the businessmen provided finances to help this family, they were inspired to provide similar help to those who were experiencing some crisis. They chose not to focus their help on people who have long-term needs, but rather those who need help to handle a particular crisis in their lives. Their motto is, "A hand up, not a hand-out." These thirty became the board of an organization now comprising 150 members. Mr. Blair informed me that last year the Nice Guys raised $1.25 million for the needy. For The Bookman alone there is a yearly fundraising banquet.

In addition to the usual agenda of helping those in crisis, several of The Nice Guys once raised about $20,000 for the work of The Bookman operation and their tradition of annual fundraising continues. Blair explained that money given to Herman's venture goes directly to the needs that The Bookman organization supplies. There is virtually no overhead. Almost all monies go to the collection and distribution of books to jails, prisons, hospitals, Indian reservations, schools, colleges, homeless shelters, as well as to schools overseas in over 120 countries. Gifts like these are crucial since Herman accepts no government funding for his operation. The relationship between these two organizations is symbiotic. The Bookman provides books to the charitable enterprises that The Nice Guys undertake.

Every year, The Nice Guys send backpacks to service personnel in Afghanistan and Iraq. In these packs they place snacks, toiletries, and a special kind of comfortable socks that service personnel enjoy. Into each pack Irwin Herman supplies a book. Service personnel at home in the San Diego area also receive the attention of The Nice Guys, who are alert to crises that often arise in their living arrangements. The Nice Guys have several programs for the military, including one that enlists the help of Navy personnel stationed on ships such as the U.S.S. John C. Stennis. Over 30 ships are involved in giving out the Bookman's books to people in port cities overseas.

The Nice Guys and The Bookman venture cooperate also in the annual Christmas party, staged at Qualcomm stadium. This book will talk about this event in a separate chapter. Ron Blair laughed as he announced the astronomical number of hot dogs he had personally cooked at this Christmas party. The Nice Guys do all the work instead of paying help to do so. I was amused at the image of an aerospace industry's CEO's flipping burgers and hot dogs for thousands of hungry children and their parents and later learned from Mr. Herman that another unlikely cook has been Mr. Rady for whose generosity Rady Children's Hospital is named. Ron Blair continued to tell me more about the organization, its aims and its modus operandi. It would be a challenge for me to remember all of what he spoke about.

As we sat sipping our coffee, I began to think of the hard work or drudgery of the whole enterprise. How was the money to be raised? Why were the 150 not weary of well doing? What motivates these persons to this noble and vast enterprise? I didn't ask Ron Blair these questions. Perhaps I already knew. They shared Irwin Herman's philosophy that one cannot provide joy to others without that joy being reflected to the provider. Is it not more blessed to give than to receive?

I discovered another secret to their long-term commitment. Blair stated that at their two annual fundraisers, the leaders try to assure that the programs are lively and fun. In the fall, they arrange a banquet celebrating the Nice Guy of the Year. No long speeches of nomination are held. The encomiums are collapsed into a twelve-minute video production. No free tickets are provided. Each dinner costs $250. In the spring, an auction is held. Unusual items are auctioned off, such as a vacation to Hawaii or a trip to the World Series. I can guess that in the dinners, the Christmas extravaganza, the planning for the distribution of gifts, the fellowship, the people of goodwill working together must shine through all these efforts.

CHAPTER 7

The Nice Guys Christmas Party
December 10, 2011

It was the largest Christmas party I have ever attended. Eight hundred families were invited to a Christmas party for those who are short of finances. Although I was not short of finances, I was invited to attend by the Bookman, who was one of the stars of the show. As you might expect, it wasn't held at a house or in an auditorium—it was held in the parking lot at Qualcomm Stadium. The party resembled nothing so much as a county fair with booths and rides and crowds of children with their parents milling around. As soon as we entered the grounds we realized we had missed the introductory remarks of Gary Tillery, who was chairman of food distribution for the party, and Rupe Linley, the 2012 president of the Nice Guys. Of course, the children were far more interested in hearing from Santa Claus than in hearing pronouncements from the party's sponsors and organizers. The Nice Guys are not interested in puffing up themselves or their organization. Santa Claus arrived in a helicopter. There were no North Pole markers on it; rather, the helicopter read, "San Diego Police Department." From the megaphone which usually announces a search for a criminal or missing child, Santa's arrival was announced. As soon as he landed he jumped into a convertible, San Diego making a sleigh impractical, and repaired to his tent with Mrs. Santa Claus where they received hundreds of requests from the children. Santa and Mrs. Santa gave the children Christmas stockings and teddy bears as a foretaste of the gifts they hoped to receive on Christmas Day.

Adjacent to Santa's tent was that other Santa Claus, Irwin Herman, smiling over six rows of book tables. The Bookman looked as pleased over the books he was about to offer as parents would be about gifts under their own Christmas trees. There was no sign indicating who was the giver of these books, so a five-year-old girl asked, "Who can I say thank you to for these three books?" A volunteer found Irwin Herman and brought him to receive the girl's thanks. He said, "Darling, you're very welcome. I hope you and your family have a merry Christmas." I thought of the account of Jesus and the ten lepers, only one of whom thanked the Master for being healed of leprosy. I'm sure that all the recipients of books were thankful to receive them but apparently she was the only one who insisted on thanking the provider.

My assistant Julie and I then spoke with Candy, a mother who had selected some books and her teen-aged son who was also holding two books. We asked them what books they had selected and what the books meant to them. Although Marcus was shy, Candy was most articulate in her responses which would do credit to a reading teacher. She stated that reading is an education in itself. It stimulates the imagination, increases knowledge and vocabulary, and enables one to travel to all kinds of places in one's mind. She also explained that, thanks to a neighborhood library and a librarian who helped her select books as a child, she became a reader and led her own family to be a reading family. The librarian supplied resources that her family lacked.

We then approached Kia, a mother who stated that she was collecting books for her three teens, a seven-year-old, and a baby whom she was expecting. She expressed appreciation for the Bookman's gift of books because, "Books cost too much." She also affirmed that, "Books are the best thing for your imagination!"

We ran into a father named Mike who had loaded a large bag of books into the bottom of the stroller that held his infant son. He was accompanied by his daughters, six-year-old Victoria and four-year-old Alyssa, who made up for their father's relative silence. "We like to read!" exclaimed Victoria. "My teacher read me a book and now I'm going to learn how to read!" Alyssa added.

Next we ran into a teen named Gilbert who had picked up three books of military fiction for himself and one other book for his sister, Isabel.

Supervising the book tables were a number of volunteers who spoke almost reverentially of the Bookman. We spoke with John, a member of The Nice Guys since 1992, Marissa, and Colandria, who noted that as the recipients of the books filed through to look at the books, they were looking for particular books. They were checking the table of contents, not simply grabbing books without paying attention to what was discussed in them. Marissa commented that people seemed to be looking for books they could relate to. Colandria told us that, "A lot of the kids are looking for Where the Wild Things Are." We ran into a volunteer named Joy Kollath, a friend of Irwin Herman's from Chicago, who was inspired to duplicate the Bookman's operation on a smaller scale in her community. We also met a retired judge whom I asked, "Why are you volunteering today?" He was more than ready with an answer. "My son, who is a Marine, lost his leg in Afghanistan and also suffered a mangled hand. Of course, he has a multitude of special needs. Somehow The Nice Guys discovered his situation. One day, some of their members appeared at the door, unannounced, with a very large check for items needed in his rehabilitation."

In the middle of all this interviewing, we heard that there were free hot dogs and sodas being served at neighboring tents. As we sat down at the table to eat them, both Julie and I remarked how delicious they were. Later we were to find out where they came from. Everything at this party was either donated by other organizations or purchased by The Nice Guys. The guests paid not a cent for food, rides, presents, free flu shots and, eventually, free bags of groceries including a frozen turkey to take home. There was even free music provided by a band, much too loudly for our appreciation, but apparently not too loudly for most of the people there. As we sat eating our hot dogs, I said to Julie, "Doesn't this whole party–the providers, the performers, and all the guests–serve as an antidote to all the negative news we are bombarded with about the country and the world?" I guess goodness doesn't make headlines or news reports. We did see police officers, though certainly none were needed. An atmosphere of joy and thanksgiving pervaded the whole grounds. Julie responded that it was impressive to see such a large number of people behaving exceptionally well as they waited in lines to receive their gifts. People were courteous to those around them and a general sense of camaraderie ruled the day.

While we were standing around the hot dog tent, we met several very involved members of The Nice Guys organization, including Mike Harland, who is involved in the Victory Fund project. He hoped to introduce us to Michael "Doc" LaMar, a former Navy corpsman who leads Operation Caregiver for The Nice Guys. We did not find Doc LaMar but Mike elaborated on their efforts with military veterans and their families through the Victory Fund.

About this time we spotted Chopper the Biker Dog, a Boston terrier outfitted with leather jacket, cap and riding goggles, who was riding around on a miniature motorcycle. We marveled at how the dog could tolerate clothing and sit on the bike his owner controlled by remote control without barking at the children. Somehow we missed Ms Smarty Plants, Pam Meisner, who, we were informed, entertained the children from the main stage while teaching them about water conservation. Apparently we missed her overalls covered with flowering vines. We learned that Kids on the Block puppeteers also provided an educational performance for the children. These puppets reflected children from all walks of life, including those with disabilities. The puppet show made children understand both their own circumstances and those of other children.

As indicated before, there were numerous booths representing services offered by sponsors. At the Wal-Mart tent the children were given materials to make Christmas cards for their families with colorful paper, markers, glitter and stickers. Running this booth was Tina, manager of the Santee Wal-Mart store, with 55 volunteers employed by various Wal-Mart stores around the county. At the art booth, sponsored by ARTS (A Reason to Survive), Diane, an expressive arts educator, mentioned that she helps people with disabilities learn to paint. At Scripps Hospital's booth we saw Les Martin, an EMT who was assisting at the booth, and Morgan and Jackie, two nurses who were giving free flu shots. Other organizations donating time, services, and money were The Home Depot, Souplantation, Al Bahr Shriners, San Diego Clown Conspiracy, the San Diego County Office of Education, Kids on the Block, Helen Woodward Animal Center, Birch Aquarium, Krusin' Kritters, Sky Hunters, Operation Game On, Project Wildlife, San Diego Humane Society/SPCA, The Burn Institute, Becky Bones, JKO Karate, Capoeira Brazilian Martial Arts and Top Flight Corvette Racing.

Although my assistant is fairly youthful, I do not possess the energy that I used to have when I attended county fairs in upstate New York, spending the whole day wandering around, watching cattle shows, riding in Loop-O-Planes and eating cotton candy. In fact, I didn't want to ride the Sky Scooper and Tilt-a-Whirl rides. I decided that I'd had enough fair for one day. As we were leaving we spotted a moving van, a large flatbed truck, and a food wagon at the edge of the festivities. We were looking at this scene where volunteers were stuffing blue Wal-Mart bags with goods when we were approached by Gary Tillery, a member of The Nice Guys and chairman of food distribution for the event. He told us that each of the families would receive two bags of groceries, a turkey and a $60 gift certificate for Wal-Mart. He explained that this was the first year that the Feeding America organization was involved with the party and they had donated use of the mobile food pantry, some of the food and 1,500 lbs. of fruit and vegetables.

Most of the participants seemed reluctant to leave, waiting until the very last minute to end their time at the fair. As happy as the children were with this day, I imagine The Nice Guys and the Bookman were even happier.

CHAPTER 8

Stone Walls Do Not a Prison Make

When I set out to write this book I knew that the most difficult part of it would be to get the reaction from some of those people who were the recipients of the Bookman's books. How do I find these people, these readers? How do I get them to state exactly what impact these books had on them? I collect glass-framed snatches of poetry and display them on the walls of my home. One of them is inscribed with the oft-quoted poem by Henry Wadsworth Longfellow-

I shot an arrow into the air,
It fell to earth, I knew not where;
For, so swiftly it flew, the sight
Could not follow it in its flight.
I breathed a song into the air,
It fell to earth I know not where;
For who has sight so keen and strong,
That it can follow the flight of song?
Long, long afterward, in an oak
I found the arrow, still unbroken;
And the song, from beginning to end,
I found again in the heart of a friend.

I am also reminded of the recent book written by the author who tried to locate all the rubber duckies swept off a freighter into the Pacific Ocean. He, of course, was curious about where the currents had taken these toys. His investigation took many months and he was only partially successful in tracking them down. It might be harder to track the books and their impact on the readers than it is to track these rubber duckies and find out where they ended up. Years ago my friend, Diane, and I wrote a message and put it in the Mohawk River, hoping that someone would find the bottle, open it and respond. Where, o bottle, art thou? Has someone read our message but failed to respond? Or perhaps the bottle lies in the sludge of some river bed or ocean floor. Perhaps it's in the Marianas Trench.

Another challenge presents itself. How does one determine the impact of a book on a reader? The Bookman has received thousands of letters. They're on his walls and in boxes. It is obvious from the letters that the Bookman displays on his walls that some of these arrows have found their mark. One gathers from them a genuine appreciation for the books. Unfortunately, beyond saying thanks they are not very articulate in spelling out just what the books have meant to them. A group of teachers from a school in the Philippines wrote letters that repeatedly thanked the Bookman but did not spell out the impact that the books had on the recipients at the school.

I would say, furthermore, that while many of the responses are from teachers, social workers and other distributors of the books, many more are from the readers themselves. I am sure that many recipients of the books never think to thank the Bookman for his gifts, but those that do are most appreciative, as witnessed by many boxes of hand-made thank-you cards. As I look back on my childhood I am ashamed to observe that I didn't think to thank my parents or my aunts and uncles for the gifts they gave me. I guess I just thought everything appeared as a matter of course, like the rain or the sun. Nor did I thank my teachers when I got to college. When I think how freely the Bookman gives these books and in what beautiful condition they are, I see that he certainly deserves more thanks than he gets. In fact they are in such good condition that I would be hesitant to give them out. Not so the Bookman.

Many of the recipients seem to lack the language ability to express just what the books have meant to them. Really, only after wide reading and perhaps formal instruction can readers find the language to convey the exact impact the books make. John Keats, in the "Fall of Hyperion," says that most men could write their feelings if they had the power of language. At the opening of "The Fall of Hyperion" he expresses this sentiment well:

Fanatics have their dreams, wherewith they weave
A paradise for a sect; the savage, too,
From forth the loftiest fashion of his sleep
Guesses at Heaven; pity these have not
Trac'd upon vellum or wild Indian leaf
The shadows of melodious utterance.
But bare of laurel they live, dream, and die;
For Poesy alone can tell her dreams, --
With the fine spell of words alone can save
Imagination from the sable chain
And dumb enchantment – Who alive can say,
"Thou art no Poet – may'st not tell thy dreams?"
Since every man whose soul is not a clod
Hath visions, and would speak, if he had lov'd,
And been well nurtured in his mother tongue.

My next step was to go out into the field to see where the books were both delivered and read. Since the original impetus for the Bookman was to provide books for those incarcerated, I set my sights on visiting those in jails and prisons. I met a blank wall. I was a bit puzzled about their impenetrability since years ago I was a volunteer teacher at the Idaho State Penitentiary. Therefore I was at ease about going into a jail or prison setting. I don't think I needed to be prepared for any such visit. I would know what to expect. I knew, too, that books and writing had a tremendous impact on some of the prisoners. At first some of the prisoners thought I was a spy for the warden since I asked them to write about themselves. It took several weeks for them to realize that I was no such thing.

I taught classes in which there were murderers, bank robbers, drug users, and exhibitionists. I remember in one class the bank robber refused to talk to the exhibitionist. Obviously he thought he was several degrees more noble or righteous. I remember the title of one essay that was written—"I See." In it the prisoner talked about a complete change in his view of himself in relationship to the world.

I was even honored by the men at the prison school with an award they cooked up. And so, I was given the Egghead Scholar Award, an award I deeply appreciated. Consequently, I was relaxed about interviewing prisoners inside the jail walls. Such was not to be. I decided to make a valiant effort to enter a prison and interview the recipients of The Bookman's books. After all, for years the Donovan State Penitentiary has been receiving The Bookman's books. Two prison libraries are named for his parents, the Minnie Herman Library at East Otay Minimum Security Jail and the Harry Herman Library at Baily's Maximum Security Jail.

I knew that one doesn't simply walk into the nearest jail and start interviewing prisoners. Those prison bars keep people out as well as in. We are aware that outsiders can bring drugs, weapons, or instruments of escape into places of confinement. From the student activities desk at Point Loma Nazarene University we heard the name of Juan Laguna, a librarian at Donovan. When I called the number for Juan a Mr. Cliff Bushim answered, identifying himself as one of the librarians at the penitentiary. He suggested that we visit on a Thursday. We, therefore, set up an appointment with him for the following

Thursday afternoon. Mr. Bushim gave directions to the penitentiary and my assistant, Julie, checked out these directions on Google Maps.

On Thursday, June 2, 2011, we drove on 805 South almost to Mexico, turning onto 905, and finally to the road leading to Donovan State Correctional Facility. The scenery around us reminded us of the line from Shelley's Ozymandias–"The lone and level sands stretched far away." We could not find a parking place anywhere near the employee entrance. Since we could not, we parked illegally on the wheelchair strip next to a disabled parking spot. We were a bit worried that we would end up inside as prisoners, committing this illegal act. As we entered the gate building for employees, we kept running into burly, uniformed men coming and going from the prison buildings. The guard at the gate called Mr. Bushim. Before we could enter the visitors waiting area, the guard made Julie cover herself with a large, white, paper garment since she was wearing the wrong clothes. Her blue jeans and blue blouse were too close to standard prison attire. The guard at the desk reluctantly allowed us to enter the receiving area to wait for Mr. Bushim.

Soon Cliff Bushim appeared. He was a small, quiet, pleasant man and he welcomed any question we had about the libraries and the people who use them. Mr. Bushim is the law librarian whose job is to provide legal materials for the inmates, all of whom are permitted by law to have access to legal books for two hours a week, according to Bushim. He supplies them with paper, pens, and other materials if needed. Sometimes they swamp him with their demands. He told us that the six libraries at Donovan are under the supervision of its Correctional Education Programs department. The librarians make an effort to maintain library hours during the inmates' recreational time. The material he gave us really offered no surprises, except for the fact that the most constant users of the library's fiction collection are people known as the EOP's, prison jargon for eccentric outpatients. He described these people as emotionally and psychologically abnormal.

Typically, prisoners come in asking for specific authors and titles and Cliff observed that they didn't care to hear recommendations from the librarians. Among the prisoners who frequent the law section of the library were prisoners who thought that they had been tried unfairly, had their sentences extended unfairly or were being mistreated by the guards. Gay and transgender inmates often told Cliff they were targets of abuse and felt they were not given enough protection from the general population.

Cliff talked about his own preparation for the job. His bachelor's degree was in business, followed by a master's degree in library science. In the future he dreams of going back to graduate school and becoming a man of science, possibly a researcher or teacher in Biology. He knew very little about the Bookman. I consequently urged him to visit the Bookman's organization on El Cajon Boulevard. He knew that most of the books in the library were donations and mentioned that Juan Laguna picks up many books from a store known as The Bookmark. Although Cliff reported that he enjoys his job, I did not detect in him a passion for the law librarian position but my assistant, Julie, commented that he smiled warmly and agreed that his job is an important one for the prisoners. He mentioned that there is considerable concern that state budget cuts will reduce the number of hours the prisoners have to use the libraries. It seems to me there is a considerable amount of folly in cutting back on these services to the prisoners.

Our big disappointment was that we were not allowed to interview the prisoners themselves. I wondered whether any of the teachers or librarians ever had an interview like one I had at the Idaho State Penitentiary when I was a volunteer teacher. A young man said to me, "My sentence will be finished in two weeks– but I'll be back."

Rather indignantly I asked, "Why would you violate your parole and be re-incarcerated?" "Oh, I'll probably get a job at a motel restaurant as a dishwasher.

When I see the boss roll in driving a Cadillac, I'll lose it and try to rob the restaurant."

I responded, "Did you ever hear of Henry David Thoreau's book, 'Walden' in which he describes his retreat for two years to a cabin he built on Walden Lake in Massachusetts? There he lived on less than $3 a year, but responded to life so amazingly that he wrote one of the best books of all time about his experiences. You don't need a lot of money to live life meaningfully. You don't need to rob a restaurant and get back here in the penitentiary."

Another prisoner responded to the prison school in an essay–"I see. I see through our reading here that the world is much broader than I'd imagined with opportunities to make life meaningful."

A third prisoner said to me, "Do you know why I like reading books at this school?" I waited for his answer to his own question. "I used to be unable to go to chapel because the other prisoners would laugh at me. After reading books in this school I've had the courage to do what I wanted to do and what I felt was right, ignoring the laughter of others."

In reality I don't think I had to get into the Donovan State Penitentiary to see the change that reading and writing brings to the prisoners there. In fact, I had the advantage of seeing not only one interview but the long term effect of books on prisoners. From that experience I became convinced that there's no better way to change the mindset of those who get in trouble than the access that language provides, both reading and writing. I have no doubt about the power of literature to change people, in or out of prison.

A prisoner whose broken glasses Mr. Herman took to the repair shop wrote a letter to express his appreciation for Herman's efforts–

Dear Mr. Irwin,
Hi, my name is Edward. Personally I owe you a lot because I enjoy a good

book whenever we had free time. I am really moved to know that someone on the outs[ide] is looking out for us by donating all the books and magazines that we have on our bookshelf. Time would go by so slow without any reading material. Your doing us a big favor by going out on your spare time and buying all the books without expecting anything in return. All of unit 700 would like to thank you in person, but since we can't, we feel good writing you this Thank You letter. You might think we just destroy the books, but about 95% of us do go to our room and read a good book. We appreciate everything you do for us so much that on Wednesdays, when we have church, we ask the Lord to Bless Your Heart because you're an angle looking out for those young men in Juvenile Hall. One of my favorite past times is writing and when I found out your name and you're the one donating the books, I just couldn't resist writing you a letter of appreciation and of sincer gratitue. Thankyou again Mr. Irwin.

Your Freind,

Edward

We got no further in trying to interview prisoners in the city jails. I contacted a Mr. Bruce Bishop, a correctional counselor at the city jail who seemed eager to be interviewed; however, he had to check for permission from his superior. He suggested that we meet at The Coffee Bean, the coffee shop almost catty-cornered from the city jail on Broadway in downtown San Diego.

He was familiar with Irwin Herman. In fact, he and his wife had dinner at the Herman household years ago. He remembers the Bookman delivering books down at the Bailey Penitentiary, where Mr. Herman gave motivational speeches to the prisoners.

The most striking thing about my interview is the information that there is no money for books for prisoners in this city. If the prisoners are to read, the books will have to be given as gifts. Currently someone from the commissary picks up boxes of books from The Bookman's warehouse and they are given out with other items from the commissary to local jails and prisons. When the supply of books gets low, Mr. Bishop orders more. The books are put in a day room from which prisoners are allowed to take them to their cells. He estimates that about 50% of the men read the books. These prisoners like a variety. The most prominent selection is for books by current authors like Grisham but there is also popular demand for law books. For security reasons only paperback books are distributed to the prisoners.

I asked Bruce Bishop, "Why do you think most people are in the jails here?" His answer was, "Poverty. Poverty often encourages people to resort to alcohol and drugs. It is also connected with the drop-out rate in schools." He cited the example of a prisoner from Los Angeles. When the young man was growing up he joined the police cadets. To stay in the organization, however, he needed to buy a uniform. Since he had no money for the uniform, he dropped out of the cadets organization. While playing with guns he accidentally shot and killed his friend. Mr. Bishop wondered if the uniform had not been required, and if the prisoner had had money, would he have ended up with a long jail sentence? I asked Mr. Bishop whether the prisoners were bitter. He said no, they were depressed.

Teachers from Grossmont College are hired to provide classes which enable the prisoners to get a GED certificate. Classes in anger management and drug addiction are also available. I asked, "Do the men talk about the books that they are reading and indicate how the books have helped them?" Apart from writing thank you notes to the Bookman, the prisoners do not articulate a response to receiving books. It would certainly be nice if they could or would.

I managed to make an appointment with Mrs. Stone of Correctional Alternatives at the Edgewater on March 7, 2012. Although she is now directing Correctional Alternatives, she is new at this job and is not party to any receipt of the books received from the Bookman there; however, at two previous locations she had witnessed the effect of the Bookman's books. At one, parents received books to be read to their children. She believes that, "Children cannot rear children." She noted that many parents more or less abandon interacting with their children as soon as the children are out of grade school. I guess the idea is how can you guide children when you are a child yourself as far as mental experience and ability go.

At another location children were offered books, which they devoured. They read until the books fell apart. At her present location, when families come to interview family members who are prisoners, someone is there to read books to the children while they wait for their parents. Mrs. Stone is most emphatic about the importance of reading. She noted that reading supplants experience when that experience is lacking. Growing up on the island of Guam, she knew nothing about sidewalks, shopping malls, skyscrapers and so forth. Reading books made up for the limited possibilities of experience that she possessed as a child. She noted that for many children, their awareness of the world and the possibilities it offers them for their own fulfillment are extremely limited. It might be that all they see is poverty, drug dealing and crime. (Hey, there's another world out there!) She noted that at the institutions where she worked there was practically no money for books. If the children were to read, books would need to be donated and, of course, donor number one is Irwin Herman.

It didn't take long to see that her job was her passion. She spent a number of years working in insurance but it lacked the challenge and excitement of seeking to improve people. She agreed with me that it's extremely difficult to get into jails or prisons to talk to inmates, nor did she offer me access to the prisoners at her institution. These prisoners look for work during the day and then must return at night to confinement at the Correctional Alternatives halfway house. Most of them never finished high school.

CHAPTER 9

Into the Highways and Byways

We had much better luck entering the homeless shelters of the city of San Diego and interviewing the people there. Books from the Bookman appear at all three venues that we visited. We started with the winter homeless shelter sponsored by the city.

I found the directors shelters much more accommodating than those at the correctional institutions. On my second call, I got through to Bob McElroy, who operates the San Diego homeless shelter. From his first word on the phone, I could tell that I was in luck. His voice exuded friendliness, optimism and decisiveness. All that I needed to say to get his cooperation was that I was writing a book about the Bookman. He told me that he, a Christian, and the Bookman, a Jew, were really on the same channel–that is, to help people is their meat and drink. He let me know that I could catch him Monday afternoon between 1:00 p.m. and 3:00 p.m.

I caught a taxi to Newton Street where the homeless shelter stands. I had figured that it was in the heart of Logan Heights. To my surprise, it is a block away from the main trolley station in San Diego. After the taxi driver located the address, he got out of the taxi and led me to the entrance. My assistant, April, met me there. Almost immediately we met Bob McElroy and he led us into the complex. As we entered, a truck departed carrying some homeless men who were headed out to work for the city. The driver and Bob exchanged greetings. There was also a young woman who Bob announced was a reporter from KPBS.

"Let's go inside and get out of this odor." The honey buckets were being emptied. I think Bob called them "shithouses." As we entered the building, McElroy said it had been a city administration building of some sort and that much work had to be done to clean out the shrubbery and set up the building for occupation. I had figured it was some old warehouse with unpainted walls, but found that the building was a painted, cheery, open space. Everybody was trying to speak with Bob. As we entered the office, a homeless woman barged in, cussing wildly, complaining about the water in the showers, asking the reporter and me for cigarettes and money.

In a kindly fashion, Bob said to this disheveled woman, "You've been drinking, haven't you?"

"No," she replied.

"You can't fool me," said Bob, "I'm an alcoholic. You've been drinking. How has your day been?"

"Terrible," she replied, "like every other day." It took considerable coaching and an offer of cigarettes to extricate her from the office. After the woman left, Bob explained to me that this woman was reared in an upper middle class family in Point Loma. Alcohol and drugs had ruined any expectations of a meaningful existence.

Like the Bookman, Bob treated me with a torrent of language and information. He informed me that he operates seven Alpha Houses, which are hospices for the homeless. Often when it rains the homeless get wet and if they can't dry out, they become ill and they die. "You've seen them die in the streets," he commented. Indeed, I had. He also operates seven shelters to the homeless in seven different cities, most of them in southern California.

"Tell me about yourself," I asked.

He began, "I used to be handsome, and I played football [I couldn't get out of him where he played football]. Sports equipment businesses used me to advertise their wares on television. These advertisements were viewed by millions of people. The only thing I had on my mind was chasing women. The thought came to me that a great place to chase a woman would be in church. I then started attending Horizon Fellowship. In a way I can't describe, God said to me, 'Either change what you're here for or leave my house.'"

The moment seems to have been a turning point in his life, for he started reading the Bible and devoting his life to be like Christ in serving humanity. He said, "I don't preach with words; I preach with my life." Jesus said, "If you want to know if I am Christ, watch what I do." Jesus then went on to feed the hungry and heal the sick.

McElroy began this work by renting an office on 5th Avenue, an office which also served as his residence. From there, he went out to contact the homeless with the object of finding work for them. I told him that I wished to interview some of the people who are benefitting from the Bookman's books. Immediately, a staff member said, "Fred is the one you need to talk to! He is lying on his bunk reading at this moment."

They showed me one bookshelf on which stood books and other objects delivered by the Bookman, including pens, paper, etc. "What percentage of the people here read the books that the Bookman brings?" I asked. I couldn't get the answer quite straight, but it was 25% or more of the men; apparently the women don't frequent the bookshelf. I thought then of the words of Bob McElroy who said that the women are far worse off here than the men. They are much easier prey for thieves and other men who abuse them. These women cash their governmental checks at a liquor store and are often robbed as soon as they leave.

While I was interviewing Bob McElroy, April interviewed a woman named Beva. She told April that although she had dyslexia she could read. Her favorites were science fiction books. She also liked practical books on home maintenance. She complained that as soon as books from the Bookman arrived there was such a rush to get them that the books she wanted had been claimed by someone else.

As April was talking to Beva, Fred arrived. Fred did not appear like a homeless person at all. He was a trim, well-shaven and clean man whose demeanor was dignified and polite. It took only two sentences from him to let me know that he was also an educated person; I can tell from the vocabulary a person uses. He told me he has an associate's degree. His brother is an adjunct teacher at Johns Hopkins University, and another brother is a wealthy business man. Although it was not obvious from the sight of him, he had suffered health problems. The scars from his mother's abusive discipline are still on his body. He has had a number of operations, including two on his back and one for prostate cancer. At present, he has neuropathy in his feet. His wife and daughter had been killed in an automobile accident many years ago.

"How did you get interested in books?" I asked.

He let me know that it was not at school or college. He got a job at an isolated gas station between Washington, D.C., and Annapolis, Maryland. Since there was neither radio nor television there, in desperation he took to reading, and he has never stopped. He reported that he reads voraciously. He volunteered that in his locker at the homeless shelter there are three books: the Bible, the works of Shakespeare, and the complete works of Edgar Allen Poe. Even the Bookman can't keep up with his reading needs. He visits thrift stores to buy more books.

"Where do you stay when the homeless shelter is closed?" I asked.

He said, "My two friends and I stay on the streets in downtown San Diego. The police know we are there. They don't trouble us, and we don't bother anyone else. We get meals at the senior center and the Neil Good Day Center."

I didn't hear him express once a desire for improvement of his situation. You would think that reading all those books about the possibilities of life that are pictured there that he might have some kind of yearning for a better life. I detected none.

"Excuse me for asking," I said, "but where do you go to the bathroom when you are staying out on the streets?"

He replied that there are public restrooms and restaurants. Occasionally the three of them rent a motel room to shower and clean up and rest. On $800 a month, there is little else he can do.

I asked him what kind of impact books had on his life. He struggled to formulate an answer. I said, "Would you agree with John Henry Newman's description of what a liberal arts education gives to a person? Newman stated that a liberal arts education imparts an acquired illumination that no one can take from you." He agreed that Newman's formulation was correct.

"Do you ever share that wisdom with anyone?" I asked.

"I try," he responded. "Once in Los Angeles, I was acquainted with a woman who was a heroin addict, but had tried desperately to get off that addiction. One night she overdosed and died. Her mother asked the pastor of the church she attended to conduct the funeral. The pastor answered, 'I will not. In effect she committed suicide by taking too much heroin, and she is now in hell.' To the distraught mother, Fred said, 'She no more committed suicide than Jesus did going toward Jerusalem, even though he knew he was to die there. And what about soldiers who go to battle, even though they are likely to face death?'" Needless to say, his words comforted the mother, though I doubt they had any impact on the pastor.

Knowing that the interview was coming to an end, I asked, "Would you be interested in being part of a little reading group to discuss books?" At first he hesitated, and then he said yes.

"How do I get to the trolley stop?" I asked Fred.

He replied, "I think I have time before serving the evening meal to walk you there." He then proceeded to guide me down the street and over about four railroad tracks even though he had advised me that he was unsteady on his feet. This guy was totally relaxed in talking with me. He seemed to have no agenda except being friendly. He certainly wasn't like that drunk woman that tried to bum cigarettes and money off me, but then he was obviously in his right mind, and he read books—that says a lot about a person.

I wonder what else I will find at the homeless shelter besides this woman with mental problems and this man who seems to live an orderly life. Fred doesn't seem to need any help reading. I am sure a challenge is to interest those who don't read to read. It is one thing for the Bookman to provide books; it is another thing to create a hunger in the homeless to read them. When I volunteered to help, Bob McElroy said, "We need all the help we can get." I am also thinking about McElroy's statement that it costs $22 per day to perform the services that the homeless shelter provides. The city only provides $12 of that. I ask myself, "Is that a good percentage of giving for the city?" Reportedly there are 8,000 homeless people on the streets of San Diego. I noticed that Bob McElroy kept mentioning the Neil Good Day Center as another facility for the homeless. I didn't know who Neil Good was, or exactly what the center did, although I knew that the center received a steady flow of books from the Bookman. It's not far from the winter homeless shelter and it's just up the street from Saint Vincent de Paul Village.

On this rainy Saturday, I took a taxi to the Neil Good Day Center on 17th Street. The taxi driver could not find the building, even though I had the address. I told him to ask somebody, and the man he asked pointed across the street. The taxi driver led me to a courtyard. As one entered, there was a table of sorts. I figured I was supposed to check in. I announced I was there to interview people about books that the Bookman delivered.

"Oh, you're the Bookman," said the staff member.

"No, I'm not the Bookman; I'm writing a book about the Bookman."

The porter to this gray area resembling Dante's limbo responded, "We knew you were coming, but we didn't know you were blind." He was looking at my mobility cane. What blindness had to do with my visit, I could not understand. The porter was a large man with a huge orange shirt. How would anyone know if he is a homeless person or a staff member?

I said, "I am not totally blind; I am legally blind."

He then led me to the building itself. This building reminded me of a small city bus station. The two places are not entirely distinguishable in my mind. Another resemblance to a bus station was that they all seemed to be waiting for something. Waiting for Godot?

A large TV screen faced five rows of chairs that stretched mostly from one end of the building to another. The general hubbub of the viewers blocked out the sound from the TV screen. The voice of what we called in the army the "bitch box" barked that no one was allowed to save seats. I sat in what I thought was an empty chair in order to interview a man. The man sitting next to the chair protested that I was sitting on his bag.

I replied, "I'm sorry. I'm blind." He should have known that since I was carrying a mobility cane.

"Okay. I didn't know you're blind," he said.

The bitch box then announced my presence, inviting anybody who read the Bookman's books to come talk to me. Several responded. Most of those I talked with seemed to have given up hope to escape the limbo they were in. There was a construction worker whose attitude was more hopeful. He was temporarily out of a job and looking for work. He had been looking for two years. Most of those

I approached answered my questions with a minimum number of words. It was as if there was a cost for every word. Their answers were not much louder than a whisper. They seemed to have lost any spark of life. Abandon hope, all ye who enter here.

One of the ones who volunteered to be interviewed, Michael, explained that he had received a football scholarship to Notre Dame. Early in the season, he was injured. Since he could not handle the academics, he dropped out. He told me he had done some radio announcing and some TV commercials. He did have a deep resonant voice.

"Perhaps I should become a teacher," he said.

"Well, you could start taking courses toward your career at City College," I replied.

He failed to respond to that suggestion.

"Where did you sleep last night?" I asked.

"Under a bridge with some others," he informed me.

All throughout my interviews, periodically the bitch box shouted instructions and information.

"All men who wish to have showers should line up at this door."

" All women who wish to have showers should line up at the other door."

"They're serving BBQ chicken one block down the street." [They do not serve food at the Neil Good Day Center].

"Don't save any seats."

"In an hour, if it's not raining, you'll have to go outside while we clean."

I did not look at the staff. They either avoided me or were too busy to talk.

In the midst of this hubbub, I continued my interviews. One person told me there were hardly any books delivered by the Bookman on the shelf. Most of the shelves appeared to house stuffed animals–for what purpose, I do not know. The Bookman assured me that a load of books is brought to the Neil Good Day Center each week. It must be that they quickly disappear into the hands of the homeless.

Vicki was another lively person who volunteered to talk. Not only did she read science fiction, she wished to write science fiction. She rambled on. I could not make head or tail out of what she was saying. I tried to keep the names and the interviews separate, but could not read my own notes. I could remember the general gist of the questions I asked and the answers I received. One of the questions I asked was what books did they like to read. I was surprised that the most frequent answer was the Bible. Someone said, "I carry around the Bible that someone gave to me." The Bookman carries a supply of Bibles for anyone who cares to read one. The book preferences went all over the place, from fiction to poetry to science fiction to biography to science to history to mystery.

My next question was the following: "Where did you develop an interest in reading?" Not one interviewee mentioned school. One mentioned at home with his mother. Several stated that they became interested in reading in prison.

The next area of questioning was why they read. Most mentioned that reading entertained them or helped pass the time. Several answers, I thought, were very perceptive. One answer was, "Reading improves my use of English." Another was, "Reading helps me to understand the world." Another said that reading helped him to understand himself and his place in the world. Another said that it helps him understand people. Another said that reading helps to keep the mind working.

At the end of the interview, I asked them where they slept the night before. Most answered, "Under a bridge." I mentioned one man that I talked to about the hopelessness that I detected in the group. I said that such hopelessness brought into my mind the verse of an old gospel hymn: "Down in the human heart, crushed by the Tempter, feelings lie buried that grace can restore. Touched by a loving heart, wakened by kindness, cords that are broken will vibrate once more.

One of the interviewees, Michael, was concerned that I might not find my way back to the trolley station and he commandeered Randy, a sixty-three-year-old construction worker to guide me the four blocks to the station. When I offered him some money, he hesitated, saying, "Are you sure you want to offer me this money?"

"Yes. You have saved me the taxi fare," I replied.

Later, when I talked to Mr. Herman about my visit, I mentioned that I had shared my ideas about conducting classes in which we talk about books and writing. Several of the homeless responded enthusiastically to the idea. The Bookman said, "Just go down there and talk. The fact that you care about them will impress them, whether you have a formal class or not. They will be especially impressed that a blind person goes out of his way to take an interest in them."

I decided to make one more trip to the Neil Good Day Center. Since I'd already been there I didn't feel I needed to ask permission to make a repeat visit. Rather than taking a taxi this time, I thought I'd get to the Center by trolley and on foot. Along Imperial Avenue, several men standing around assured me that I was headed in the right direction. Somehow I overshot 17th Street and ended up on the thruway. I wondered why there were no sidewalks along the road. Some guys yelled, "Hey, you're walking on the freeway!"

I replied, "I'm trying to get to 17th Street to the Neil Good Day Center."

The men directed me back to 17th Street.

At the barrier someone snarled, "You had an appointment last week, not today."

I just stood my ground. Another person, apparently the attack dog superior, said that I might go in.

I said, "I'd like to interview a staff member, please."

"I have no time for that," was the answer. "Talk to someone at the desk."

I could see that a woman was behind the desk, studiously avoiding talking to me. I got the hint that I was not welcome and moved on to interviewing those homeless people that agreed to be interviewed. There were probably half as many people on this sunny day as were in the center a week ago when it was raining. Again, they sat there, in what seemed to me like a stupor, watching the large TV. One man refused to be interviewed; several didn't know anything about the Bookman or his books. About four answered my questions. I was really learning nothing new except that a couple said that they had gotten interested in reading in school or at home. One man stated that he became interested in books as he rode with his father, who was a trucker. Generalizations are very dangerous. The ones I had made about where these homeless had become interested in reading proved inaccurate.

Again, we were all ordered outside for cleaning purposes in the room. One of the homeless men led me to a table and found me a chair. John approached the table. He seemed eager to be interviewed. He began his answers by saying he didn't like junk books. I asked him why he read. He answered, "Apart from entertainment, reading keeps the mind supple, and it makes one sensitive to the world around him." He was interested in reading books by authors like the Brontes and Dickens. He asked me who my favorite writers were. I answered that my favorite prose writer was James Boswell and my favorite poet was Percy Bysshe Shelley. I informed him that I was writing a book about John Keats. He wanted to know about the relationship between Lord Byron, Percy Shelley and Mary Shelley.

He continued, "My teachers said that I was stupid. They didn't like the fact that I contradicted some of their statements."

I replied, "Those teachers did you a disservice. I can tell you are very bright. What plans do you have for your life?" I continued.

"I received training as a pharmaceutical assistant," he offered, "but they won't hire me since I have had no experience."

I responded, "What about becoming an–" I stumbled at the word.

"An intern," he responded.

"What about attending City College," I suggested.

"I don't have any money, and it costs money to take courses there," he said.

I tried to encourage him to apply there anyway and see if they could find a way for him to attend classes.

"I have to leave," he said, "but are you coming back next week or sometime?"

Next, a sixty-year-old man named Isaac approached. He was a steady reader. Again, I asked what he got out of reading. Apart from entertainment, he said that reading broke down barriers of prejudice. He added, "The more we find out about other people, the less judgmental we are of them." Quickly he got on the subject of religion. He was reared in a Christian home, but has since tried Hare Krishna, Mormonism, Buddhism, and Islam. He is still interested in Buddhism.

I asked him what plans he had for his life. He replied that he had appeared before the City Council several times. He rather shocked me by saying, "I choose to remain homeless. That's the way I wanted to live." I didn't pursue the subject.

He, too, wanted to know whether I would return and, out of nowhere, asked me to pray for him. I gave him my *In Spirit and In Truth* book. He then introduced me to a man, saying that I was interested in questioning him about the Bookman. The new arrival said that he did read some of the books and that his children did also. Trying to be polite, I asked, "How many children do you have?"

"What has that got to do with the Bookman," he snarled.

"Nothing," I said, and he stalked off.

To two of the men, I showed a sheet on which appeared Simon & Garfunkel's song, "Bleecker Street." One man started reading the footnote at the bottom. I began to recite the first stanza of the song.

"What do the authors say about Bleecker Street? Do they like it?"

"Yes," he responded.

I responded, "Do you know what a shroud is?"

"No," he responded. He didn't seem interested in exploring the poem anymore.

The second man to whom I showed the poem again thought the authors were praising Bleecker Street.

"What does it mean," I asked, "when the poem says that Bleecker Street hides the shepherd from the sheep?"

"Well," he answered, "I guess there are sheep in New York City." He, too, did not seem interested in pursuing the task of unpacking the meaning of this poem.

About this time, I was surprised by how tired I had become and asked Isaac to lead me across the street. On the way back to the trolley station, I stopped at Saint Vincent de Paul. On entering the door, I was confronted with an iron fence.

"What do you want?" a voice called out.

"I would like to interview some of the people who read the books that are delivered here by the Bookman," I responded.

"Call on Monday. Here is the phone number," he responded.

And that was the end of my visit to the Neil Good Day Center. I concluded that it wasn't just on Bleecker Street that would-be shepherds were hidden from the sheep. At least the visits to the Neil Good Day Center inspired me to write a poem.

Limbo At Imperial (Avenue, That Is)

One stop, two stops–
Green light.
No pay on Broadway.
One block, two blocks, three blocks–
Green light.
Civilage at Father Joe's Village.
One knock, two knocks, three knocks–
Four cops.
Red light.
Front porch to the city.
Walking, talking, swirling, purling, smoking, doping.
A queue of cars.
Hi, Angel, queen of the caravan.
And the homeless bowed and prayed,
To the neon god the Neil Good Center made.
People looking without seeing,
The vacant stare.
Poverty, inebriety, neuropathy, pathology, pathos, pathetic.
We were building a stairway to heaven.
Someone slipped and fell.
Oh, hell! The Slough of Despond.

We cannot find the steps, O Evangelist (aka social worker, counselor, do-gooder).

Here we sit like birds in the wilderness,

Birds in the wilderness,

Birds in the wilderness.

Here we sit like birds in the wilderness, waiting to be fed.

Books from the Bookman,

Water from the Waterman,

Preachments from the Preacher Man,

Counsel from the Council Man,

And a few bucks.

Here we sit like birds in the wilderness, waiting to be fed--

Bread,

Bed,

Head,

Sped,

Dead.

CHAPTER 10

And Gladly Teach

Saint Vincent de Paul Center–March, 2011

"If you can read this, thank your elementary school teacher." So read the bumper stickers we used to see here and there. I am well aware that except for autodidacts, putting a book in a person's hand is not sufficient. A person needs to be taught how to read. While most people–even the homeless–have an elementary school education and know how to decode words and sentences, they often do not know how to really understand what they read. Learning the art of understanding the printed text should be a lifetime pursuit. The goal of every reader should be to improve his or her ability to grasp what the author is saying and to apply it to one's own life.

The Bookman's organization depends on other philanthropic people and institutions to enable those who receive the books to read them intelligently. I applaud the Bookman's endeavor to supply books. I feel the impulse to enable recipients of the books to read them well. I tell my students, "It takes two to tango." We have no question about the ability of the great works to dance; we have questions about the ability of the readers to participate in the dance of meaning. It was the truth of the importance of the teacher that urged me to volunteer my teaching at the Saint Vincent de Paul School.

I decided to visit Saint Vincent de Paul and carry out the idea I mentioned at the Neil Good Day Center of discussing books in an informal class setting. Ever since I moved to San Diego in 1979, I have heard about the Saint Vincent de Paul Center for its work with the homeless. I heard bits and snippets about the place, including that there was a residential program there and that the Center provided meals for the homeless.

On March 17th, I decided to visit to interview those who read books that the Bookman sent. I had set up an appointment with Nick Coniairis, director of career and education counseling. Since I cannot drive I plotted my trip to Saint Vincent de Paul. I walked up Imperial Avenue from the trolley station, and after entering the building for low-rent housing, I was directed to the main building next door. The lobby could well have been that of an expensive hotel. There were huge arched windows and ceiling lights and seats for waiting. About six people were sitting quietly. I decided to fill up the time by asking some of them whether they read books provided by the Bookman. Two responded with a curt "No." One woman exclaimed delightedly that she had sent a letter to the Bookman thanking him for two of the books she had read. She wished me to pass greetings on to him. Another man said that although he did not know there were books provided by the Bookman, he had found a medical book and read it.

While I was interviewing these people, a man rushed through the front doors exclaiming, "A woman is lying on the street!"

One person asked, "Is she drunk?"

Another asked, "Is she conscious?" About four men rushed out to handle the situation.

At 1:15 p.m. I decided to have the receptionist give Nick a call, since the appointment had been set for 1:00 p.m. A few minutes later Nick arrived, calling out for Arthur. I explained to him that I had not mentioned my visual handicap to him on the phone since it is only a part of my life and not the most important part, by any means. I was tremendously impressed with both the physical environment and the activities of the educational center. In one room

Nick explained that the people were studying how to handle their emotions. In another room students were receiving tips for landing a job. In the main instructional room about thirty people were watching an informational television program and filling out workbooks in response to what they had seen on the screen. The atmosphere was quiet and serious.

Nick took me into his office and answered questions. First I asked him questions about himself. We found out that we had both received master's degrees from Boston University. In various jobs with social service agencies Nick had found himself unchallenged. Therefore, when he heard about the job opening at Saint Vincent de Paul, he applied and was hired, even though he took a pay cut. He explained that all the wonderful facilities there existed because the shelter operated from a twenty million dollar annual budget. He also explained that the organization had built from the bottom up, not from the top down. In other words, the buildings and the programs evolved as the need presented itself. The Center is not the embodiment of someone's fancy. There are 800 full-time residents and thousands that avail themselves regularly of the services offered by the Center. Before becoming a full-time resident, people must undergo a screening and a kind of boot camp. It takes a while for some to curb their alcohol or drug-related problems. Some must learn to temper their freewheeling lifestyles. As soon as they enter the shelter itself, they must enter the psychological help and educational program of the Village.

I knew that I was just discovering the tip of the iceberg of this complex and wonderful organization. The program reminded me a bit of my own basic training for the U.S. Army. Individuals had to surrender part of their freedom in order to improve their lot in life. In other words, there is no free lunch. To me it certainly did not seem like party time at the Village. My guess is that many of the residents had been participating too much in party time and that had led to a number of dead ends. Many of them obviously needed structure. I wondered, but had yet to discover, how many homeless people are turned away. I had heard of a man who left his wife and family to wander like a savage around Balboa Park. I suppose he thought he was experiencing freedom, not knowing that freedom can impose its own chains on one's life.

One thing that surprised me was the absence of any overt religious symbolism or presence. I saw no crucifixes and met no people in religious habit. I had talked earlier to the chaplain, who, to my surprise, was a woman. I had felt surely that the chaplain would be a priest. I suppose I was thinking of the old model of church-related foreign missions in which homeless were treated to a meal only after listening to a sermon. Perhaps such a regimen just makes "rice Christians." While they say that the best way for a woman to a man's heart is through the stomach, it may not be true that the same principle works for religion.

Nick went into one of the nearby classrooms. He had announced to the class that I wished to interview anyone who had read the Bookman's books. One man responded immediately that he had read books on psychology.

Back in the office, Nick brought in a tall Haitian man. Nick said, "Isn't he handsome?" He looked like a basketball player to me. The man not only gave his first name, Anthony, but his last name, even though I asked only for his first name. He was currently reading a self-help book from the Bookman's shelf. He found reading the book very helpful. He explained that he was temporarily out of a security officer job. Next, Nick ushered in a middle-aged woman who announced herself as Patrikia. I began by complimenting her on her pretty name. She mentioned a daughter who had graduated from a prestigious college. She liked detective novels and murder mysteries. Responding to my question about why she read, she answered that reading for her was a pleasure. The books helped her to relax. I was pleased to hear that a third grade teacher had turned her on to reading.

After this visit I decided to volunteer as a teacher at Saint Vincent de Paul and, over lunch, discussed my plan with Nick. He proposed an hour session after the regular instructional period. This session would be strictly voluntary and therefore he suggested I provide cookies as an enticement to those who would stay for the reading and writing class.

The day came to teach my first class. Loaded with cookies, cider and my tape recorder I headed for the center. After exiting the No. 7 bus at San Diego City College at Broadway, I boarded the crowded, rackety trolley headed for Imperial Avenue. No one volunteered a seat for me and the announcement system was not operative. I had to ask three different people the names of each stop. Finally I staggered off the trolley and found my way across the tracks and a side road to Imperial Avenue. Since I had only visited the school once, I asked two men outside the building how I could enter the school. They were too busy talking to each other to answer my question. I asked a lady who then led me to the school building, up the stairs and into the office of Nick Coniairis.

I arrived at 2:00 p.m., although my class was not scheduled to begin until 3:00 p.m. Almost immediately I was met with three students. Angel and her husband, Chris, and Amy, a friend of Angel's, seemed very eager to talk. I began asking the questions I usually ask of readers of the Bookman's books. Angel reported reading a spiritual book about how to know the voice of God. Amy was reading "The Testament" by Paul Grisham. Amy reported that her fiance, who is a painter, pored over art books contributed by the Bookman. She said, "He spent so much time looking at them I began to wonder if he would wear out the books."

Amy reads an average of six books a month. Is it any wonder that she passed the language part of the GED test with flying colors? Only math was holding her back.

I was impressed with how clean and attractive was their appearance. Amy reported that her mother interested her in reading while Angel reported that she learned to read from a teacher in school. She even remembers the teacher's name. Angel wanted to know if I was the Bookman.

"No," I said, "but I know him."

"Do you know the Water Man?" she asked.

"Who in the world is the Water Man?" I responded.

"Oh, he's an elderly gentleman like you," she replied. (I didn't like being identified as elderly at all.)

"He provides port-a-potties and distributes water to the homeless," she went on.

I said I wanted to meet this man. She fumbled around for his business card but could not find it. Then she called 411 to get his phone number. There were too many David Rosses in the phone book for her to have any success.

Angel's husband, Chris, a strong-appearing man, stated that today he was to have an interview with a corporation that might hire him as a security guard.

I replied, "Well, I'd hate to tangle with you."

I found out that Angel has three grown sons. She has spent some time in jail–for what I have no idea and was not about to ask her. Amy's fiancé is receiving drug counseling, she reported. Amy showed me a poem she had written and she read it to me.

Loneliness
By Amy
Loneliness leads to heartache
Way down the road of simple lust.
To put it up, it all at stake,
A simple tear, a total must.
Teardrops form a river,
No way to travel for non-swimmers.
Raft required to escape.

Teamwork to build a life.

Hand-n-hand we survive.

Angel's husband is a painter and has sold a few paintings. We were enjoying this three-way conversation when someone came into the office and said the class was waiting. There was no Nick around to introduce me to the class or to tell me that it was about to begin. I, therefore, walked in and began to teach. I told all 12 of them that they could call me Doc. I tried to play Simon and Garfunkel's "The Sound of Silence" on the CD player but it kept returning to the beginning. Angel told me she would select the correct song on the CD player. She also passed out the sheets with the words to the song. I began to ask questions that would explicate the song lyrics, like, "What time of day is the setting of the song/poem?" "Where are the 10,000 people mentioned in the song?" and "What does it mean to talk without speaking, or hear without listening?" and "What is the neon god they worship?" and "What are the words written on the subway walls and tenement halls?"

I gathered that most of them, anyway, had no idea what the poem meant, largely because they didn't understand metaphor. I, therefore, told them. Perhaps that is not the best teaching strategy–I don't know.

I said, "I've been over to the Neil Good Day Center and have seen rows of people staring blankly into a huge TV set, the sound of which could hardly be heard above the noise in the building. As I remembered I became impassioned at the waste of human opportunities that I had witnessed at the Center. I guess being passionate about my ideas is my trademark. Perhaps it was one of my college students who called me "Chalk Dust and Tears." He also informed a student teacher that I was the one among the faculty to be imitated.

All the students listened carefully. They were most well-behaved but the conversation was not lively. That is, perhaps, my fault. At 3:45 p.m. Angel passed the cookies around and I then told them they were free to leave. Some did immediately. Some sat in their seats. Several asked whether I was returning every week. One gal clapped after I ended my talk. Unfortunately, none of the rest joined in.

There was no Nick around but Angel offered to walk me to the trolley station, holding my hand as we paraded down the street. I do believe that Imperial Avenue, which runs in front of the Village, is the friendliest street in town. A number of people greeted Angel as if she were a long-lost cousin.

I left wondering how much these people understand in the books they read.

My Second Class at St. Vincent De Paul

It was a hot day. I lugged, on the bus and trolley, two bottles of apple cider and a box of bakery cookies. This time Nick led me to a comfortable chair in the classroom rather than to his office. The only person I recognized in the classroom was Constance, who proved to be my assistant in the absence of the previous week's assistant, Angel. (My angel had flown away.) Nor was the poet Amy there. I think Constance was the only one from the previous week's class. This week there were only eight in attendance–all women except for one man.

We listened to Simon and Garfunkel's "Bleecker Street" and I took the whole time explicating the song with them. I realized how much background information they lacked. For example, none had ever been to New York City. Nor had they seen West Side Story so they were unable to see where Bleecker Street was (as the poem says it is near the East Side bank). I forestalled any kind of question about sheep and shepherds on Manhattan by indicating that there were none and, therefore, the reference was metaphoric. The Romanian woman on my left said, "It is like a parable." Certainly the words about fog covering the men sleeping in the alleys helped them to see that the poem was about streets like Imperial Avenue in San Diego on which men sleep.

One woman knew that a shroud was a cloth but I had to supply the information that it was a cloth that covers a dead body. They were very good when discussing a shadow touching a shadow's hand, stating that these were the dead. When it came to knowledge of a sacrament they were very weak; also on Canaan. I had to prod them to relate the $30 with the 30 shekels for which Judas sold Jesus. Once they understood the song, they were very interested in it and the whole subject of homelessness.

I was very moved by the story of the Romanian woman, who had obviously experienced homelessness. She also indicated that alcohol had played a part in it. "Without money, or a job what else could I do?" she said. From the very lively discussion I got some explanations for homelessness. First, some homeless people want no rules or responsibility. Second, many of them lack a good education and this lack hinders them from getting jobs and knowing how to cope. Third (mentioned by the Romanian woman,) Americans don't respect older people. They don't keep them as part of the family. Fourth, they have lost hope. Fifth, the high price of housing. Again, the Romanian woman said, "I'm not paying a thousand dollars for an apartment!"

One thing that bothered me about the discussion was that no one asked me about the way out of the homelessness dilemma. I said, "The last line of the song saddens me a great deal. 'It's a long road to Canaan.'"

I am beginning to wonder whether continuity is a wished-for mirage down here. I wanted to build on the previous week's writing by talking about making general statements based on details. Perhaps this is like how a preacher or evangelist feels. He has to strike carefully and hard because his sermon may be the only one some of the audience will hear.

My neighbor suggested that the enthusiasm that some expressed the previous week was like a flash of light rather than a continuing beacon. I am a bit discouraged. There were only five or six in the class yesterday. On the other hand, they were all enthusiastic participants in the discussion and they all, except for the Romanian woman, read with polish and verve.

At the beginning of our next class meeting, a small young man asked if this was the literature class. I said it was and he asked if I was the teacher. "What is your name?" I asked. His reponse was, "Plain Hope." I wondered if he was a Native American. My bet is that Plain Hope needed a literature and writing class badly, but he melted away somehow while the women, who have rather strong language skills, remained.

I had decided to vary their diet by having them read a novel–"The Summer I Was Lost" aka "Terror on the Mountain," by Philip Viereck. I started "The Summer I Was Lost" by saying that, although it was a young adult book, anyone can profit from it. The message in the book is far from juvenile. I also mentioned that I had taught this book with college students and at the Idaho State Penitentiary. To tie their experiences in with the experience of the 8th grade protagonist in the book, I had them write down their failure experiences. We revisited last week's discussion on the causes of depression.

Since several people at the Neil Good Day Center mentioned that they lacked Bibles, I secured some from the Gideons organization and passed them out at the end of class. Caroline was the only one who wanted a Bible. One person said, "Good class." I noticed again that there weren't many regular students around. The schedule of classes at Father Joe's is a puzzle to me.

Last week, during the class, a young woman stood at the bookshelf with books donated by the Bookman, leafing through a book. I asked her what it was and learned that it was a memoir. The words of a Christmas carol come to mind–

How silently, how silently the wondrous gift was giv'n.
So God imparts to human hearts the wonders of his heav'n.

I can write "How silently books work on the human imagination." If one is a teacher, he or she must be patient. Often many miles must be walked before one stumbles on a signpost indicating progress. Somehow I feel that the five women in yesterday's class had made great progress somewhere along the line. I have high hopes for their futures.

(One exception to this rule took place in British literature class. The assignment for that day was to read James Joyce's short story, "The Dead." In the middle of the class a student stood and reported, "This story has changed my life.")

The next week as I faced my third class, I did not feel like going to St. Vincent De Paul to teach. If it weren't for some of the wonderful, faithful students there, I would have quit. When I arrived, the guard did not want to let me in because I did not have a badge. Somehow I got in anyway. As I sat waiting for the class to begin at 3:00 p.m., a young man stuck his head through the door and asked, "What about this writing class?" The resident teacher at St. Vincent De Paul indicated me sitting there–"There's the teacher." The man looked at me for several seconds and withdrew, saying nothing. Apparently he expected to see some beautiful damsel instead of me.

Mirable dictu! Angel and her husband returned to class. She said they had been through a lot in the last month. Someone accused her of hiding a liquor bottle under her mattress. I don't know what else had happened to them. Two new men attended. One volunteered to read and he read very softly. He did not participate in group discussion. The other man, Glen, was a writer. He told me that although he was able to get a lot of writing jobs he could not hold down a job because of depression. He added that he was about to have a book of poems published. I asked him if he had any of his poems with him. He did. When he read one I was astounded by his description of a homeless woman. He'd never thought of writing a memoir and reported that he would return to class another time.

Angel told me she'd spoken to the Waterman about me and had obtained his phone number so that I could call him. He told her to have me wait a week because he'd been injured in a fall and had a split lip.

The class was suspended when I went for my summer vacation back east. I failed to renew teaching the class when I returned. For one thing, Nick Coniairis was no longer head of the education department and I had trouble getting in touch with the new director. Then I succumbed to a certain kind of discouragement. One day in the spring I had gone with treats, ready to teach, and was told that the place was locked down for bug eradication. No one told me that classes would be suspended that day. Then I bought notebooks for the students, encouraging them to write memories of their childhoods. Apparently no one did. I never knew who would be attending the class.

Yet I feel a certain twinge of regret at not renewing the teaching. Basically, they were hungry to learn—some more than others. I, too, was learning from them about people with different backgrounds and different circumstances. I believe that if I'd had a class of twenty or more students I might have continued. Then, too, I have many projects outside of teaching that I'm pursuing, including writing this book.

CHAPTER 11

Straw for Making Bricks

It is surprising that educational institutions, one of the main purposes of which is to introduce students to books, often have a dearth of books. We are starving in the midst of plenty! Every year there are more than 50,000 new titles of books published in the United States. (Water, water everywhere and not a drop to drink.) And yet, teachers are asked to make bricks without straw; they are asked to enable their students to become literate, but lack an adequate number of books with which to complete this task efficiently.

Frequently we hear accounts of teachers who are forced to buy materials for their classrooms with their own salaries. As you might imagine, Mr. Herman is very eager to supply the books needed in educational systems around the world. His scope is broad—from preschool to college, from San Diego to the world.

Virtually all recipients who are teachers or social workers record their amazement at the generosity of the Bookman. My own irrational response is that these books are so beautiful and wonderful that I would hate to part with them. Not so the Bookman. Nearly all the books he distributes are in top-notch condition. They might as well be new. For example, a friend of mine who teaches elementary school students, Michelle Gates, was rather sheepish about taking 17 boxes of books from the warehouse. Of course, the Bookman was very firm that these books are to be given away and not hoarded for any personal library. I am amazed that he will donate huge container loads to be sent to foreign countries without charging one cent.

The Bookman's warehouse is crowded with letters saying thank you, but rarely do they articulate more specifically just what the impact has been on them. We expect a better response from teachers and students in school. I asked Michelle Gates to describe the impact of books on her elementary education students. Here is a letter she wrote.

In August 2011, Art Seamans took me to a literary treasure trove. The name of this incredible resource is "The Bookman," a warehouse floor that is filled entirely with books. There are cookbooks, travel books, children's books, teaching books, student texts, math books—every kind of book.

As an elementary teacher who works mostly with struggling students, I found myself in the proverbial candy store and was quickly set loose to search amid boxes of words. As a resource teacher, I had a definite intention in my foraging. I have spent the past five years working with students who are performing at less-than-grade-level standard and are pulled from class to meet with me to strengthen their reading skills. These students struggle with everything from decoding to fluency to comprehension and need books available at their varied levels.

I also work with other teachers who are trying to build up their classroom libraries in order to enhance classroom learning. As the economy has been increasingly painful for classrooms and teachers, classroom and school libraries have been negatively impacted, with the most often enjoyed books becoming worn and needing replaced but no funds available to do so. My hunt was for books to enhance ailing classroom libraries and for books that would address reading deficiencies while still teaching subject matter to students.

Classroom library books—While at The Bookman, I found books for four different classrooms.

 For a second grade classroom, I found Leveled Readers, addressing basic decoding skills, as well as early chapter books for fuller comprehension. The teacher who received these books uses them for "Reading Counts" tests, which are comprehension building quizzes the students take on the computer. After reading 20 books, the teacher rewards students with a trip to the prize box to help positively reinforce their reading efforts. Each student has a goal for reading a certain number of books a month and receiving a certain percentage correct on each test. The Bookman's books are building comprehension while encouraging student interest in reading, since they get to pick from a wider range of books in the classroom.

For a sixth grade classroom, I gravitated towards The Bookman's Newbery Award winners. These are children's books that have been honored for their writing, receiving a Newbery Honor or Award. The teacher whose class library was enhanced by these books had recently needed to purge her library of numerous books that had been worn and damaged due to overuse. Her class is using the books in two ways–Accelerated Reader program and Literacy Circles. The Accelerated Reader program is similar to Reading Counts in that it is a comprehension oriented assessment program which tests students using computer generated tests. To promote student engagement and comprehension, Literacy Circles are used by this teacher to provide students with specific foci while reading a book with other students. In Literacy Circles, there are various jobs–questioning, summarizing, illustrating, defining, coordinating. The team of students works together to read small portions of text and help each other develop a more complete understanding of the book. The books in this classroom are directly impacting student comprehension as students read to learn and be able to interact with each other, adding to the learning environment of the whole class.

A middle school English teacher was the recipient of other Newbery Award winners. Her students have been using these books for independent reading and book reports.

A middle school History teacher found herself teaching sixth grade social studies for the first time. This year is focused on ancient history–Rome, Greece, early hominids, Egypt, Israel–and was a topic area where she had very few resources. "The Bookman" not only had books that substantially fleshed out her meager library but also had videos that have presented her students with another avenue to access the information.

Resource books—For intentional, focused development in areas of student weakness, "The Bookman" provided many resources.

I am currently working with first through fifth grade students who need specific intervention in their reading and language skills. Some of my students need comprehension skills, others need help in basic decoding, while a few others need intensive work in English Language Development.

I am meeting with a young man who has only been in the States speaking English for one year. His lack of English is currently hampering his development in all other English-related topics (science, social studies, reading, writing, speaking). However, in his native Portuguese, he was a proficient student, which indicates that English is truly what is standing in his way to academic success. To meet his vocabulary development needs, I have provided him with reading materials two years younger than his current grade level, focusing on expository text that strengthens his academic concepts while providing reading he can access and academic vocabulary that helps him in class.

I am providing after-school tutoring for a group of fifth graders who are testing Below Basic and Far Below Basic on their annual CSTs. One of the focuses of the program being provided to this group is the enjoyment of reading. For this reason, we have an intentional, independent guided reading time where students choose from a batch of teacher-selected books and get the opportunity to read these books. While the group of students is reading, I sit with different students, having them read to me to assess their fluency and asking questions to spot-check their comprehension. I have had to bring in books that not only meet their reading abilities but also their reading interests, which are varied. "The Bookman" provided me with expository texts that the young men in my group devour and with animal stories which the young ladies squabble over. It has been a joy to see these students absorbed in books, especially knowing that, in the past, it has often been a fight to just get them to read.

Further exposure—I have been telling every teaching friend I have about "The Bookman," encouraging them to seek him out or to spend a few hours just wandering the halls of his treasure room, finding the many precious gems that he has hidden there. In fact, I just returned there this past Friday, as my English Language Learning young man has gone through the books I got for him in August and is in need of more to feed his ever-growing vocabulary and desire to learn.

Michelle Gates, Resource Teacher–City Tree Christian School;
Impact Teacher –Emory Elementary School; and After-School Intervention
Teacher–Lincoln Acres Elementary School through UCSD Extension

I am acquainted with a high school teacher, David Penn, who took books from the Bookman for his 11th grade English class. He kindly showed me his students' written reports after reading the books. Their reactions to reading a particular book are articulate and impressive. We culled some comments from a selected number of their book reports.

Brandon Paulus, in his review of *The Call of the Wild*, wrote–
The reason Jack London would write a book like this is because he is trying to demonstrate that you should always follow your true nature and not live a life you were not meant for.

Reviewing *The Maze*, by Will Hobbs, student Kyle Rayder wrote–
F. Scott Fitzgerald stated "a single defeat is never a final defeat." That is the idea that I think Will Hobbs was trying to present. This book proves that it's never too late to change the direction of your life.

Olga Ruiz wrote about *The Mall* by Richie Tankersley Cusick–
I think the author…decided to write *The Mall* because it's about how liking someone can turn into an obsession, and being obsessed with someone is never good and it can even turn dangerous.

In his review of *The Terrorist*, Chris Brock points out–
Caroline B. Cooney has multiple reasons to write *The Terrorist*. The main reason is to show how characters can change.

Rashaan Souikane read *Imaginary Enemy* by Julie Gonzalez. Of the main character, Jane White, she wrote–
The main conflict in this story is about how she fits in, she is very conscious about what people think about her. Jane will have to come to a point in life where she either accepts her own actions or continues blaming them on Bubba…When I finished the book, I closed it and left the room with a happy face.

Samiira Hussein reviewed *Harry Potter and the Sorcerer's Stone,* writing–
Harry Potter and the Sorcerer's Stone, by J.K. Rowling, is an inspiring book about how an ordinary boy discovers he has much more to live for…The author went away with her thoughts and imagination while writing this novel. Rowling's book outlines every young adult's test of becoming a unique individual, deserving respect from people, learning about loyalty, discovering the difference between pardonable vices and unpardonable sins, and believing in something bigger than oneself. Harry transformed from a neglected orphan living under stairs in a closet into a famous individual, and then into a young, brave hero.

Irwin Herman makes it very clear that he is ready to fulfill any request he can from a school that wishes to expand its library holdings. The most prominent recipient of The Bookman's books is the San Diego City College. Every week a van from the Bookman goes to the long line of tables outside the campus bookstore to fill with books of all sorts. Herman complains that the students don't offer to help him unload the books, but I tell him that they would if asked and I was told that he is known as a hero on campus for his gift of books.

I decided to see the operation firsthand. I called the Bookman to see whether the weekly delivery trip to City College was on. I was disturbed to hear that instead of departing at the usual time, the book van was leaving in fifteen minutes. Hoping to meet the van as it unloaded the books at City College, I rushed to catch the

No.7 bus. I asked the driver to let me off at City College, but he mumbled the stops, and a man and woman ten seats away were yelling at each other with their conversation. Taking a lucky guess, I got off on Park Boulevard at the right stop. Once on campus, I was surprised to see what a beautiful campus it really is. I guess I expected it to be a place where functional buildings stood. I asked two students how I might get to the library. Tad offered to take me there.

"Do you see any books lying around here?" I asked. Since he saw nothing like what I was looking for, we asked the librarian, who informed us that the books were delivered outside the bookstore, not the library. As we walked, Tad informed me that he was a veteran of the war in Afghanistan. Obviously he had survived the war intact and with a helpful and gracious spirit. There we discovered a long row of boxes of books on tables. They stretched about thirty-three baby steps along the way. The books were all packed in with only their spines showing since there were so many of them. There must have been hundreds of books there. I reached in to feel the books. They felt new, clean, and unused. For an hour and a half I stood observing as a parade of students filed by, examining and taking books. I was surprised at how unsociable and serious the students seemed. There was little interaction among them. That observation worries me.

I have learned to be quite bold in approaching people. It takes a bit of screwing up one's courage to speak to strangers but if you have to, you have to. I suppose I asked about twenty people questions relating to their presence at the Bookman tables. A couple told me that they were too busy to talk, being in between classes. One student refused to give me even his first name. "I might be misquoted," he offered as an excuse. Isn't it sad that some people have learned to be so suspicious? Did he think I was a policeman, or an FBI agent? I told each student that I was endeavoring to write a book on the Bookman. Most did not know who he was. One called him a "fantasy person." Another called him "an angel." The tall man who offered to lead me off campus said that the Bookman was a legend on campus, a hero.

Three of the people with whom I spoke were professors of sorts. One young man told me he worked with a basketball team. He was collecting books to give to them. A sociology professor said that he was collecting children's books to give to elementary schools in Mexico, where children were trying to learn English. He also gives books to his wife, who in turn offers them to the single mothers she works with. A third professor informed me that occasionally he brings his class to look for books. Another man takes books to his business class, where there is a sort of library there. One young lady named Sheila collects writing books for her sister, who has aspirations to become a writer. Another young woman collects books on handicrafts, again for her sister. I was struck with how many were taking books not for themselves, but to give to other people. One young man held up a paperback with the title How to Become a Hero to Your Younger Brother and Sister. He had a big grin on his face, so pleased was he to find the book. As I said before, I stayed there for an hour and a half observing a steady stream of people perusing the books. I have no idea how long this went on after I left. Over the years the outreach of this venture must be tremendous.

The man who helped me off campus said that he collected books on electronics. He told me that though the books were not entirely up-to-date, they were helpful to his fellow class members. Only one person, a young woman, was looking for novels. Others like Hector wanted books on psychology, sociology, mechanics, reference works and biography. I thought to myself, I keep hearing in the media that books are passé. The continual flow of young people, eagerly pawing through books, argued against that position. People love books.

I wondered why almost all the people who trooped by looking at the books were mostly men. Maybe I just came at the wrong time. I made another observation. Each person spoke softly, answering only the questions I asked. They seemed subdued somehow, almost, may I say, lost. It is dangerous to jump to broad generalizations. Neither the people I met at the homeless shelters, nor the people at City College seemed to be particularly interested in the possibility of a book being written about this whole venture when I told them that was the purpose of my being there.

Another locale where I could examine the impact of the Bookman's books is Point Loma Nazarene University. Since I still share an office at the university I didn't need to travel anywhere for my investigation. Dr. Jim DeSaegher picks up books from the Bookman for his yearly book and bakery sales benefiting the literature, journalism and modern languages department. It is not surprising that the Bookman and Dr. Jim DeSaegher would join forces at some time since they both have a passion to collect and distribute books. While Dr. DeSaegher was teaching he started a banquet for graduating seniors majoring in Literature and Journalism. Jim DeSaegher took delight in getting acquainted with his students. He loved trying to make the undergraduate years meaningful to the students he taught. His wife, Lou, once told him that she must have happily cooked over 300 dinners for majors that Jim had invited over to the house. After students ate a delicious home-cooked meal they often stayed around the house playing board games and socializing with each other and the DeSaeghers.

In the same spirit of bringing professors and students together, Jim and former Literature, Journalism and Modern Language Department Chair Noel Riley Fitch instituted the Senior Banquets in 1982, a tradition that continues to this day. Each graduating student receives a book gift at the banquet. One thing led to another and when it happened that funds were low for the banquet Jim decided to first hold bake sales to raise funds and later added books to the sale of baked goods. Sales are typically held four times a year. Between the Literature building and the student center Jim sets up tables loaded with books and fresh donuts. Professors donate books for which there was no more room on their shelves. Soon others heard about the need for used books and donated some of their books to the sales. To increase the amount of books, Jim and Lou scour thrift stores and library book sales for bargains, closing sales at bookstores, and discarded books at public and university libraries. After conferring with students,

Jim set a price limit of 75 cents for each book. Today the book sale typically brings in approximately $900 a year.

Dr. DeSaegher had another purpose behind these book sales. He believes that everyone should have a personal library but especially those who end up teaching. Jim calls English teachers eclectic pursuers of knowledge and it is true that English has ill-defined boundaries with psychology, history and even the natural sciences. While to aid their teaching English, teachers could resort to university or public libraries, there is much to be said about possessing a book in one's own library. I didn't ask him this question but I know what his answer would be. Does not an educated person love to have books somewhere in his or her environment?

Like the Bookman there lie reasons behind DeSaegher's passion to teach and distribute books. He reports that he early became an avid reader since an asthmatic condition kept him from pursuing outdoor sports. He would read up to six books a week from the age of six. It is interesting to note that reading books has provided him with enough knowledge that one of his high school English teachers who had low vision offered him a job grading the papers turned in to her. In his undergraduate work at Westmont College Jim was drawn toward majoring in music or psychology. When a new English professor, Ken Richardson, began teaching at Westmont Jim found his other interests subsumed under his love of literature.

Jim DeSaegher enjoys knowing he's helping students get a start on their personal libraries. Graduates who went into teaching often took some of his books from the sales to supply their classrooms. A group of students from PLNU even took books from the book sales over to Africa to help start a library one summer.

The Bookman feels free to try his humor out when Dr. DeSaegher visits to pick up books. He has nicknamed Jim DeSaegher "Curly," doubtlessly because DeSaegher is mostly bald. Knowing that DeSaegher taught at Christian universities, the Bookman sang, "Onward Christian Soldiers" as DeSaegher climbed the steps to the Bookman's floor. The Bookman now supplies many of the books for the DeSaegher book sale. Recently he has sent over many religious books. While it is true that a Christian college has an interest in religious books, DeSaegher must let the Bookman know that any liberal arts college must have an interest in subjects outside of religion.

Children in schools are voluble in their praise of the Bookman, as we saw in the many boxes of letters they have sent him. We only had the energy to go through one of the boxes. Irwin Herman especially enjoys letters from children. Two young fans from a local elementary school wrote the following letters which are displayed in the foyer of the Bookman's warehouse, along with their classmates' letters and photos.

Dear The Bookman and Lenny the Elf,
I have heard that you two are going to give our class free books to read. I think that sounds great. Anyway, I do need education like my parents say. I think just hearing you talk must be a great thing to do if I had the chance.
Your friend,
Dominic Figueroa.

Dear Bookman and Lenny the Elf,
I really aprishat what you are doing. I think you guys are doing something really nice to schools, prisons, and for orfens. I see lot of people trying to buy out of us, but you guys are donating it to us. Thank you for the books and good luck.
P.S. I like your name.
Sincerly,
Juan Benitez

The following letters represent a sampling of the hundreds upon hundreds of letters written and mailed as well as notes jotted in the Bookman's log. He invites visitors to write in the log when they come to select books. Most notes we found were from instructors and teachers representing various schools or community programs.

Thank you so much! It's my first year teaching 3rd grade at a brand new school. Last year was my first year teaching kindergarten and the books I got from you made up the majority of my class library. I came back for my 3rd grade class and I know it will be very helpful to both myself and my students.

Thanks again!
Christin Hwang
Aspire Inskeep Academy, South Los Angeles Area

I feel ALIVE and ready to read! THANK YOU!
Catrina Price
International Rescue Committee, San Diego

Thank you for opening my eyes to the business of helping people. Keep the books in motion!
James Hunt
University of San Diego Graduate Student

Thank you so much Mr. Irwin Herman for donating books to children in the Philippines. These children will help other children when they grow up. As what you said—paying it forward. More blessings. Reading changes people!
Rainier Pabuna
Happy Fish Kids Learning Center After School Program
Purok Mangingisaa Fishing Village, Philippines

Dear Bookman Hero,
Thank you, as usual, for the wonderful books for my students. I have several students in my classroom who do not have books at their homes and I know they will love them. You make such a difference in my—our—lives.
Thank you.

Meghan Walsh
Special Education Teacher
Highlands Elementary School

By the grace of God, I have found Irwin, the Bookman, who is a
remarkable man who is donating children's books to the African Library
Project. Victor is working with Southwestern College to collect a total
of 1,000 books in which African Library Project will assist to send these
books to Lesotho. Books donated will be going to Lesotho in Southern
Africa. The district in which the books will arrive is in Bothe-Bothe.
Victor Cuevas

If you come across "Algebra for Dummies," please save it for me. It's my
third attempt at college algebra.
THANKS!!
Richard from San Diego County Mental Health

One of my goals is to help develop a small library at Safe Haven downtown.
It is a place that helps homeless people get back on their feet and resources
are limited. I feel that by providing good reading material for them, they
are encouraged to read and I have found that many people there do read
the books I bring and I feel good about it. Thank you so much for being
available to provide these people with books to stimulate their minds and
give them the hope because some people in the world do care.
Sara Schell

Not only are the books great Mr. Irwin is greater.
Kevin from the MAC

I feel that the bookman is what this world needs. Without the help of the
bookman my son's library at school would be non-existent. Thank you for
the support.
Jeremy Marr
Magnolia Science Academy

You devote your life to helping others. Your support in providing books
to Presbyterian Urban Ministry is a great service to the homeless. They

can experience travel, scripture and all kinds of life otherwise out of their reach.
Hank Copeland

Bookman,
I cannot believe you exist! This is an amazing resource for the community. I have lived in City Heights for 16 years and am glad to know that you and your elves are here to support young readers. Thank you for all you do.
Blessings,
Angel Ramon
YMCA Learning Program

You have touched the lives of so many children—and with all the books I've taken, many more will be touched.
Thank you.
Vanessa Escarcega

Mr. Bookman was not only very giving but full of humor. It was a great experience to meet him and see the huge collection of books. Thanks so much for supporting the East African refugees of San Diego.
Paige Newman
Somali Family Service

The Highwayman with his co-pilot, Shela.

CHAPTER 12

Close Encounters of a Philanthropic Kind

The Bookman is not an isolated case or individual who responds to the needs of people around them by offering them assistance. The Old Testament records that when Moses wondered how to go about freeing the captive people of Israel, the Almighty said, "What is in your hand?" Even a cup of water is praised as an offering to the thirsty in the New Testament. My investigation into the wonderful gifts of books that Irwin Herman has given to those in need has turned up some other cases for those who help the needy.

What I discovered is that there must be hundreds of good Samaritans in the city–people who, without fanfare, help those in need by giving their energies and their money. Jesus said of those putting coins into the treasury that those who make a big splash for people to see have their reward but the hundreds who do these acts have perhaps even a higher reward.

Since Angel, my student at Saint Vincent de Paul, had roused my curiosity about the Waterman , I decided to seek him out. Somehow I found out that the Water Man had an office or center on 8th Avenue near the public library. I got off the Number 2 bus and walked a block to a nondescript place where some people who, I assumed, were homeless were milling around. "I'm looking for the Water Man, I said. A young woman said, "He just left." "When will he return?" I asked. She responded, "We don't know. He's unpredictable." A month later I took the bus again and got off at 8th Street to visit him. This time I spied a desk. The attendant looked suspiciously at me before admitting that the Water Man was, indeed, there in his office but was busy. "Who are you?" she asked but offered to check to see if the Water Man was available. A minute later she said, "I'll take you back to the office so you can meet him."

Like the outer room, this inner office lacked any aesthetics that I could detect. The man behind the desk introduced himself as Gerry Limpic, the Executive Director for the Water Man Check-In Center. David Ross was preparing for a meeting with the police chief and was frantically trying to find his spectacles and notepad. At first I figured that he could not be the Water Man. I had pictured a slim man in his seventies who was obsessed with his good works but did not care for interference from nosey writers. I discovered that I was totally off and that the large-framed, friendly man standing beside me was the Water Man. At the mention of their financial exigencies, I whipped out a twenty-dollar bill, an action that pleased the Water Man, who informed me that dozens of homeless would receive water because of this contribution.

I must confess that I was puzzled that the homeless needed water. Weren't there drinking fountains around? I had not seen many and when I was thirsty I would simply stop in at a fast food establishment or restaurant. This option is not open to the homeless, who lack spare money. The Water Man asked Gerry Limpic to arrange a time when I could interview him at length.

After the Water Man left and returned several times, I began asking Gerry questions.

He began to explain the workings of the Water Man Check-In Center to me. The center is a copy of one in Los Angeles' Skid Row. The center provides a place for the homeless to leave their backpacks or carts while they conduct errands or business. He explained that the center desires to replicate a living room atmosphere. Each homeless person is greeted as if that person were a millionaire or a much-sought-after customer. In turn, the homeless treat the center as if it were their own. Neighbors notice how the whole area is upgraded because of the center's existence. The center is not allowed to distribute clothing or food or anything else. Thus, the Water Man travels around the city, checking on the homeless, offering them water, and providing them with port-a-potties. It did not take long before I discovered a spiritual motivation to Gerry's work. In earlier days he was a guitarist playing gospel music and a church music director. The staff at the center often have opportunities to counsel the homeless, even to pray with them. "This is my kind of work," Gerry affirmed. "I want to help people who are the neediest and help them at the point of their need."

I must observe that many of the people providing services to the homeless are motivated by religious concerns. Gerry mentioned that the center's greatest need is for enough money to keep the operation running. I asked if area churches had contributed but he said that none had yet responded to the Water Man's requests for funds.

Gerry had many things to do so I agreed that I would return another day for another interview.

Sharon, another student at St. Vincent de Paul, wrote this tribute to the Waterman–

The first time I met Waterman Dave he pulled up in a black car. He had a little white dog with one eye. He was handing out Gatorade and Slim Jims. He was friendly and caring. The first night of my suspension I was sitting by the JKC building. It was raining and I was cold. Dave drove by and came back to see if I was okay. He gave me a Gatorade and some crackers, a couple of rain coats. He asked me if I was warm enough with my jacket and I wasn't so he gave me his jacket and talked to me for a little while. He said, "Be safe. God Bless you!"

I've decided that the Water Man is much more interested in delivering water to the homeless than he is in talking to a would-be author. Rest in Peace, Water Man.

I discovered another practical philanthropist when I mentioned to the Cooksleys my project of writing about the Bookman and they informed me of a "Book Woman" with whom they were acquainted. I met Dorothy at a dinner hosted by the Cooksleys at their condo. I then took Dorothy to dinner at Seaport Village to interview her. It was a lively interview. During the interview I was reminded again of the quote from Thoreau–"Rescue the perishing and tie your shoestrings." Her good works spring spontaneously from her caring heart.

Sitting at the Edgewater Bar and Grill, she revealed that she had held some 70 jobs during her lifetime, including work in a third world country and being a counselor on a caravan for a 7-month trip in a Conestoga wagon for disturbed youth across the United States.

At her local library she discovered that the librarians were throwing away perfectly good books. To her, books are sacred. She loves reading. When she discovered that her local library was discarding boxes of books, she protested at the waste. Consequently, they let her take the boxes which she gives to other libraries, many of them eager to get the books, or she gives books to the homeless, or to a Native American reservation. Sometimes she simply drops off a box of books where the homeless are encamped. She wonders why the libraries don't communicate with one another about books they would like to acquire. She does not store books in her home.

Dorothy admitted that she has difficulty in just sitting still. That explains why she is a bit of a wanderer. At least once a month she packs her two dogs in her Dodge van and drives to a camping area for a few days. She ordered only an appetizer for dinner. After my main dish I ordered some dessert with her promise that she would help me eat it. Among other things that she has accomplished is working her way across the country doing whatever job she could find.

After the meal, Dorothy guided me to the parking lot since it had become dark. In the south parking lot she could not locate her car, having me stand while she walked around the parking area several times. I began to worry that the car had been stolen. I kept saying to her, "Are you sure that you didn't park in the other parking lot?"

"No," she responded. "I am positive that I turned left into this parking lot."

I suggested she present her ticket at the parking kiosk, a suggestion that proved to be very fortunate since the attendant informed her that, indeed, she had parked in the north parking lot, not the south parking lot.

Then I discovered that there was a recent college graduate who, having taught in Latin America, started an organization to provide books to the schools where she had taught while there. One morning my neighbor Richard, with whom I have coffee, brought me an article from the *San Diego Union-Tribune* about Emily Moberly. I called her and set an appointment for lunch. On January 30, 2012 I waited outside Johnny R's for Emily, whom I call the Book Girl. How was I to know that Johnny R's was closed for a Christmas party on January 30?

Emily arrived right on time, explaining that the truck she drove was her father's since her car had been stolen. I suggested we go to Coco's across the street. She easily fit the pattern of a female undergraduate student, although she is 24. She was very friendly, even bubbly. In fact, I had to interrupt her to allow myself to ask her questions since I wanted to direct the conversation. Her motto is "Never, out of fear, hesitate to do something." Thus, wishing to get away from home, she attended John Brown University in Arkansas. Her mother is a teacher and her parents eager to do good works. In fact, they took her on day trips to Mexico to help the needy. She did not enjoy these trips.

While majoring in journalism at JBU, she took a semester at a Christian university in Uganda. From fellow students, hearing that they wanted to start a library in a small town in Somalia, she secured funds to help start the library in that town. One of her classmates at JBU suggested that she apply to teach at his hometown in El Salvador. Her application was accepted and for a year she taught English and Sociology at a high school.

Although most of her students were not deprived financially, she found that they were deprived of books. They were surprised to see her reading "To Kill a Mockingbird" in her spare time. They associated book reading with homework. Most had never read a book for pleasure. Returning back to her teaching assignment from Christmas vacation, she carried a suitcase full of books and distributed one to each of her students. Most fell in love with reading the books she gave them. One unmotivated student named Walter ended up reading 11 books that year. Three of her students are now attending universities in America.

Emily noticed that in the town where she taught there was a small library and a bookstore that had virtually no good reading material. She then started an organization with some other like-minded friends, the purpose of which was to supply books to foreign countries. She has had no problem securing books but realizes that the great problem is securing funds to mail them to foreign countries. She sees churches and schools taking on the challenge by receiving donations of $100 per person. Twelve hundred dollars will provide enough money for a huge shipment of books to any foreign destination.

Since she has a full-time job in a financial institution, the running of her project must be done in her spare time. Hearing that her board meets periodically, I suggested that their next meeting be at my house combined with a pizza party.

She was very eager to meet the Bookman and to see his operation. She told me she has talked to him on the phone and received some books from him. I have lost contact with her but hope that she did get over to visit the Bookman and I hope that her small organization is successful and growing. I hope that many young people in Latin America will be beneficiaries of her efforts.

My neighbor, Richard, knowing that I was interested in humanitarian individuals, brought to my attention another article he had just read in the *Union-Tribune* about someone called the Highway Man. At first I thought it would be a story about some crime on Interstate 8 or Interstate 5, or somewhere else. The article quickly disabused me of that opinion. The Highway Man was not a criminal but a do-gooder. I looked him up on the internet, found his telephone number and called him. Yes, he would be glad to have lunch with me. On Thursday, April 19, 2012, I met Thomas Weller, the Highwayman, for lunch at Johnny R's. We both arrived early. He ordered only a bowl of chili to save me money. I asked him how he got into the highway rescue business. One blizzardy day when he was a teenager he drove his car into a snow bank and waited for help. Probably wisely, he did not set out walking to get that help. Finally a man discovered his stranded car, came with a truck and pulled him out, perhaps saving him from hypothermia or death. The man refused to take any money. Instead he said, "My payment will be that you help someone in trouble." For 40 years the Highway Man has been repaying that debt.

Another factor that caused him to get into the business of helping stranded drivers is that he worked for the Good Year company and now has an automotive repair business. God asked Moses, "What is in thine hand?" Moses said, "A staff." The Highwayman had a wrench. So both did the will of God in this world with what was in their hands.

A third motivating factor that moves him to this charity is that he finds that helping other people relieves his depression. How severe depression he did not say. Since he only works part time he has a considerable amount of time to donate to his rescue operations. The previous day he had spent five hours on the highway and assisted three stranded drivers. I mentioned that his hobby involved a great deal of adventure, to which statement he agreed. He has best cases and worst cases for responses to his offers of help. The worst case was when four toughs started jostling him for money. His companion at the time—I assure you, not Shela the Dog–fired a gun into the air, thus rescuing him. The most fortunate rescue attempt was helping a lady who, it turns out, was related to Representative Duncan Hunter. In appreciation for what the Highway Man had done for his relative, Duncan Hunter invited him to a banquet in which The Highwayman, along with others, was awarded an American Hero award and a considerable cash sum.

Occasionally drivers whom he attempts to help are frightened of him. One woman slipped the trunk key to Weller through a crack in the car window so that he could get the spare tire.

The Highwayman worried about boring me with his stories. He has tons. I assured him I was not bored. One tall, thin man in a business suit stood by his car, perplexed. Weller turned his own car around to assist the man. When Weller refused to accept money, the tall man wept. Perhaps the greatest deed he did was coming upon a car with a family of Mexicans. The car would not start and they were just sitting there. Weller ordered them to stand by the side of the highway, fortunately. A drunken man smashed into the car, killing himself. Had the family remained in the car, they too in all likelihood would have been killed. They were effusive with thanks to Weller for saving their lives.

There are some bad people out there. One highway patrol man threatened Weller with arrest if he saw him trying to assist a motorist. When he assisted a young woman and the highway patrolman came upon him to arrest him the young woman screamed at the officer at the thought of the Highway Man being arrested. Later that officer was dismissed from the force for other reasons. Most unfortunately, once when Weller stopped to assist a car by the side of the road, the woman in front of him put on her brakes. A car slammed into him from the rear. Had Shela not been in a harness she probably would have been killed. Weller got a ticket. The woman in the car in front of him probably tried to pretend to have whiplash, asking him whether he owned a company or had a lot of insurance. The accident ruined Bertha, his faithful rescue vehicle, which was a patchwork of repairs. It held a lot of equipment that Weller used in his repairs.

One group of gang members ran out of gas. When he approached the car they snarled, "What do you want?" When, to their astonishment, he offered them a tank of gas they burst into smiles and drove off.

I asked him what problems people experienced on the highway. He responded, "I suppose the most help needed is for flat tires or running out of gas." He also replaces fan belts, dead batteries, and performs other minor repairs. Two weeks ago he gave out two batteries with the promise that those who received them would compensate him for the batteries. He has heard from neither of these people.

After I persuaded Weller to have a piece of pie he invited me out to the car to meet Shela. He had gone out twice previously to check on her. The window on the car was down; he had a sun shade in the window, and had parked in the shade. Originally he had found Shela at the dog pound and when he put her in his car she immediately sat in the driver's seat and put her paws on the steering wheel as if to announce that she would be the driver. She was a beautiful dog, multicolored. She was friendly without being effusive. She appeared to be quite dignified; however, he said that when he wanted to get her attention he would yell, "Cat!" Immediately she would perk up since she loves to chase cats. She also loves to go to Dog Beach. What dog wouldn't? She was not doing well lately but when Mrs. Weller replaced her dry dog food with human food, Shela perked right up. Since she is able to detect good people from bad people, I was pleased that she gave me a couple of licks on the hand.

On the side of this replacement car, as with Bertha, there were these words –"Dog is my co-pilot," and "Lord, help me to become as good a man as my dog thinks I am."

One of his favorite places to help people is on the Coronado Bridge. He has cut back on night time assistance because of his age and his eyes, although two lenses have been donated to him for his eyes. One grateful man gave him an expensive pair of sun glasses since he wouldn't take any money for help. Of course he lost those in a day or two. He will not take money for his services yet I don't know how he is able to afford all the driving and donations of batteries and gas to stranded motorists.

Just recently my assistant reported that there was a Mule Man abroad in San Diego County. For 20 years this man has followed three mules wherever they chose to lead him. The purpose of this venture is to advertise the wonders of the outside world. As noble as the Mule Man's venture may have been, I decided not to sink from the sublime to what appeared to me the slightly absurd. I draw the line at the Mule Man and his mules. I told Julie not to schedule any kind of contact with him or with his mules.

CHAPTER 13

Philosphy of the Bookman

Heraclitus said, "Character is destiny." Glimpses of Irwin Herman's character are seen throughout these pages. Perhaps it would be worthwhile to organize both his thoughts about life and his own character, which is the implementation of these thoughts.

The first thing I note about Mr. Herman is that he is a fiercely independent person, perhaps even a proud person. Maybe that is why he takes no help from the government in running his organization. That independence shows itself in his courageousness and entrepreneurship. We have seen this in how he took over his father's business, paid the debts and built the business into a very profitable one. We have seen this in the pride he takes in his own Jewish heritage. Even as a boy he stood up to a bully who tried to intimidate him by using a slur against Herman's Jewishness. By the way, he expects that other people will have the same integrity. He gets very upset when someone tries to build a personal library from this charitable organization. One of the reasons that he enjoys the support of the Nice Guys is that for them, like him, one's word is one's bond. They do not need written contracts. There are no hidden motives in their philanthropic work. I noted that with the Nice Guys, Jack Grace, the Elves and the Bookman there is no endeavor to glorify themselves. In fact, I found the Elves a bit too retiring as they made an effort to stay out of the picture during my visits. I am flattered that Mr. Herman accepted my proposal to write this book without checking out any of the references I had provided for him.

A second characteristic of The Bookman is that he believes that actions speak louder than words. He makes no pretense of being a strictly practicing Jew. Rather, he believes that one pleases God by the nature of his deeds. At the local temple his family attended as he was growing up, he was much impressed by the words inscribed there. From Isaiah the words read, "What doth the Lord require of thee but to do justly, to love mercy, and to walk humbly with thy God." He feels that Bob McElroy and he are on the same page with showing by works rather than words the nature of one's beliefs. As we have noted, there is nothing that angers him more than people who profess high ideals and betray them with their actions. Specifically he mentions clergy who have molested children.

A third thing I would note about his character is that he loves people and life. There is a constant joyousness about him and his work. He admits the fact that his wife is in a care facility and that he himself has some major health problems. He openly expresses the sorrow he had at the death of his son. He pointed out to me that one can choose between emphasizing the problems of life or the joys of life. He does not deny the problems. He chooses to emphasize the joys. The jokes he tells are part of his desire to see life in a lighter vein than the world some people create for themselves through their choice.

It is no secret that he loves meeting the people who come to donate or pick up books. He loves honoring their requests. He delights in their thank you notes.

A fourth characteristic of the Bookman is that he strives to make his work have significance. I repeat the old story about the passerby observing some stone masons at work. To the first worker the passerby asks, "What are you doing?" To which the first worker replies, "I'm placing one stone on top of another." He asks the same question to the second workman. The workman replies, "I'm building a wall." The passerby then asks the third worker and asks the question. The third worker says, "I'm building a cathedral."

One of the reasons that the Bookman permitted me to write this book is that he wishes that many others will become engaged in some project that betters the world. Of course, he wishes that not a child or a person on the earth would suffer intellectual and imaginative destitution because no books were available. So the Bookman is not just passing out books. He sees his job as helping as many people as possible to be stimulated by reading the books that he and his organization provide.

The fifth characteristic has already been mentioned. That is his spontaneity. To paraphrase Thoreau–Don't be like the moon that goes peeping around like Robin Goodfellow; but rather, be like the sun that gives its brightness to all around. I recounted earlier how the Bookman sent a prisoner's broken glasses to be repaired by an optometrist. When he heard that Leonard's daughter in London had died, Irwin Herman immediately offered an airplane ticket so that Leonard might be able to travel there. I mentioned the toilet seat, stuffed animals and the walker that he keeps on hand at the warehouse. Every time I leave after having met with the Bookman at his warehouse on 37th Street, I find myself saying a prayer–"May his tribe increase."